THE CHILDREN'S BOOK OF
KWANZAA
A GUIDE TO CELEBRATING THE HOLIDAY

BY
DOLORES JOHNSON

ALADDIN PAPERBACKS

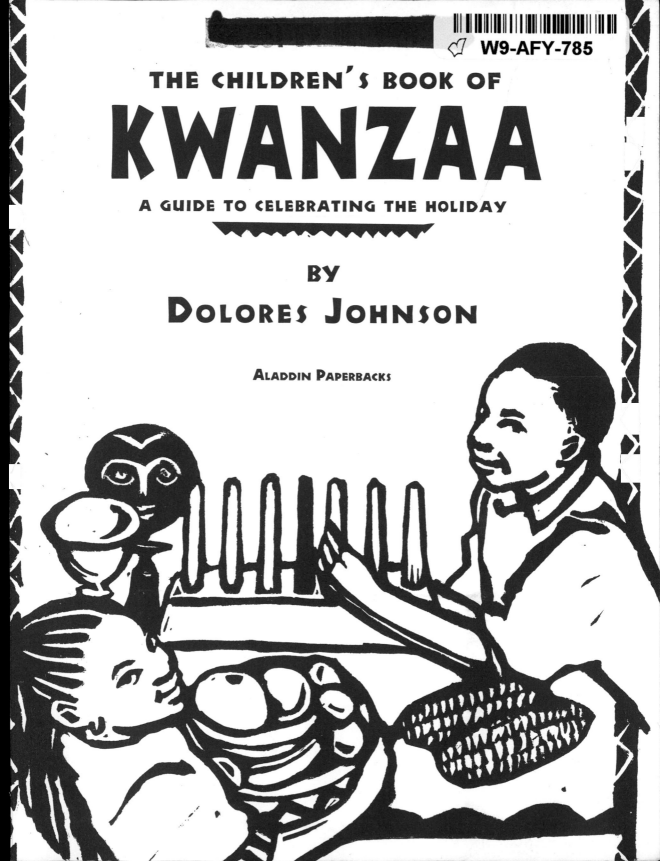

25 Years of Magical Reading

25

ALADDIN PAPERBACKS
EST. 1972

First Aladdin Paperbacks edition October 1997
Text Copyright © 1996 by Dolores Johnson

Aladdin Paperbacks
An imprint of Simon & Schuster
Children's Publishing Division
1230 Avenue of the Americas
New York, NY 10020

Also available in an Atheneum Books for Young Readers edition
The text of this book is set in Monotype Bembo.
Book design by PIXEL PRESS and Becky Terhune
The illustrations are linoleum block prints and pen-and-ink on paper.
Printed and bound in the United States of America

10 9 8 7 6 5 4 3 2 1

The Library of Congress has cataloged the hardcover edition as follows:
Johnson, Dolores.
The children's book of Kwanzaa : a guide to celebrating the holiday / Dolores Johnson.—
1st ed.
p.   cm.
Includes bibliographical references.
Summary: A guide to the origins, principles, symbols, and celebration of the African-American holiday.
ISBN 0-689-80864-X
1. Kwanzaa—Juvenile literature. [1. Kwanzaa.] I. Title.
GT4403.J64   1996
394.2'62—dc20
95-45286

ISBN 0-689-81556-5 (Aladdin pbk.)

IN MEMORY OF MY MOTHER,

WHO TAUGHT ME HOW TO COOK, HOW TO SEW,

AND HOW TO FULFILL MY RESPONSIBILITIES.

CONTENTS

THE CHILDREN'S BOOK OF
KWANZAA

INTRODUCTION

A journey of a hundred miles starts with just a single step.

—Ancient proverb

WHAT IS KWANZAA?

Kwanzaa is a celebration of the African American people, their culture, and their history. It is a seven-day festival which begins every year on December 26, the day after Christmas. On every evening of this festival, a family member lights a candle in a specially prepared candleholder and discusses the principles of Kwanzaa. The principles are about unity and purpose, and looking for ways to make the family and community strong. On the sixth day of the festival, December 31, family members and their guests take part in a feast of celebration.

HOW DID KWANZAA BEGIN?

DR. MAULANA KARENGA

The holiday known as Kwanzaa was created by Dr. Maulana Karenga in 1966. Dr. Karenga wanted to create a holiday for black Americans that was not just about black heroes or heroines (like Black History Month), but about bringing people together and reaffirming the bonds between all black people. He looked to African culture for inspiration, particularly the African "first fruit" festivals which were held to celebrate the harvest. The word *Kwanzaa* itself comes from the Kiswahili phrase for first fruits, *matunda ya kwanza.* (Kiswahili, sometimes referred to as Swahili, is the most often spoken language on the African continent.) Dr. Karenga added the extra *a* to give the word greater significance.

African first fruit festivals were known to occur as far back as ancient Egypt and were then called the Per-In-Min (Coming Forth of Min) festival. Other celebrations, such as the Ashanti and Yoruba New Yam Festivals, still occur all over Africa today at the harvesting of the new crop.

Dr. Karenga chose the African first fruit festivals as his models for Kwanzaa because he felt they generally shared five characteristics:

1. They gathered the people and the crops together at the time of the harvest.
2. They allowed the people to give thanks to the Creator for a good harvest and a good life.
3. They allowed for the commemoration of the past, especially for the ancestors.

4. They allowed people to examine their individual pasts and recommit themselves to creating a better neighborhood and community.
5. They celebrated the Creator, history, culture, and the promise of the coming year.

It was also from these African models that Dr. Karenga developed the *Nguzo Saba*, which in Kiswahili means "Seven Principles." These principles are unity, self-determination, collective work and responsibility, cooperative economics, purpose, creativity, and faith. They are the foundation of Kwanzaa. (We will discuss what these principles mean in chapter 2.)

Dr. Karenga chose the dates December 26 through January 1 to coincide with the American pattern of year-end celebrations, and to make sure Kwanzaa would occur after the usual commercial Christmas buying season. Setting Kwanzaa at that time allows participants to take advantage of the holiday spirit, as well as the feeling of renewal many desire around the new year.

WHY CELEBRATE KWANZAA?

The celebration of Kwanzaa allows African American children and their families the opportunity to explore, share, and celebrate a part of their own heritage. Other tangible goals are the beautification of the community and the strengthening of bonds among neighbors and family.

Another aspect that is special about Kwanzaa is the gift giving. Dr. Karenga determined that gifts given at Kwanzaa should teach as well as entertain; therefore, he felt one of the gifts should be a book or a heritage symbol. (A heritage symbol can be anything of African origin, such as kente cloth or mud cloth, or a representation of an African American hero, such as a picture of Harriet Tubman.)

He also felt Kwanzaa gifts should be a demonstration of love between family members and friends, and should not be given as the result of a need to buy or receive the biggest present. In fact, Kwanzaa gifts are often made by hand, rather than bought, as an additional sign of caring and affection.

But what is most exciting about the holiday is that it is relatively new, and many families have not yet created their own Kwanzaa traditions. So children can be the ones to introduce the celebration to the rest of the family. A child can help establish the traditions, make the decorations, write the songs, invent the games, make the gifts, provide the entertainment, and even help cook the food for the Kwanzaa feast.

Children can invite other children, other family members, and family friends to participate in this holiday in which they have played such a large role.

Children can also help their family, class, or organization spread the joy of the holiday to the rest of the community. For example, sometimes local shopping malls have Kwanzaa ceremonies at the beginning and end of the holiday. Children can perform in a Kwanzaa play or sing a Kwanzaa song at the community observance. Children can also lead candlelighting ceremonies at their church or mosque. Children can demonstrate the *Nguzo Saba*, the Seven Principles of Kwanzaa, to their schoolteachers and to other members of their class who are unaware of the holiday. What is now a relatively lesser known observance in this country could become widely practiced throughout the world with the help of the child.

WHO SHOULD CELEBRATE KWANZAA?

You don't have to be African American to celebrate Kwanzaa. Both black and nonblack people can participate in the ceremonies. On March 17 every year, there are more than a few non-Irish who wear green and say they feel "just a little bit Irish" on St. Patrick's Day. Non-Chinese go to Chinatown every year to participate in the Chinese New Year. Mardi Gras originated as a pre-Lenten Catholic festival, but non-Catholic people from all over the world gather every year in New Orleans and other cities to join in the carnival. Americans have often enjoyed and celebrated the different nationalities and cultures that flourish in this country.

You don't have to follow a particular religion to celebrate Kwanzaa. Nor do you have to change your religious beliefs. Kwanzaa is not a religious festival, but a cultural celebration. Anyone can observe the holiday, much as most religious groups honor Mother's Day, Memorial Day, Valentine's Day, and other American holidays.

Anyone and everyone is encouraged to use this book to create his or her own Kwanzaa celebration. Schoolteachers, Scout leaders, parents, community leaders, and, especially, children should be able to use the instructions provided in the following chapters to design their own festivities. Remember, however, that Kwanzaa is not just for children. It is an opportunity for all to study, to promote, and to celebrate the African American culture. It is also an opportunity to create something of value by hand, whether it be a simple gift tag or a book of family memories that can be passed on from generation to generation as part of the Kwanzaa tradition. The holiday, which began years ago as a celebration observed only by small groups of people, is now being celebrated by more than twenty million people worldwide.

CHAPTER ONE

A HISTORY OF AFRICANS AND AFRICANS IN AMERICA AND ITS IMPORTANCE IN THE CELEBRATION OF KWANZAA

"To understand history is to understand ourselves."

—M. Karenga

WHY STUDY HISTORY?

Kwanzaa, created as a holiday celebrating African values, also developed as a result of African and African American history. It is the struggle and achievements of those African Americans who lived before us that encouraged Dr. Karenga to create the holiday.

Much of what we are today is the result of the struggles of those who came before us, regardless of our racial identity. Perhaps by understanding who our ancestors were and how they struggled to achieve our present status, we can appreciate what must be done to create a better world for ourselves and future generations. Perhaps by understanding that we share so many common bonds, we can help to solve our common problems. Dr. Karenga said: "One is morally compelled to remember the struggle and achievement of the ancestors. For it is they who paved the path for the living and the yet–unborn. . . ."

WHO ARE THE AFRICANS?

Very little has been written about the people of Black Africa in American and European history books. But in fact, Africans were some of the world's first peoples. The oldest remains of ancient man were found in Africa.

For thousands of years, black Africans lived as farmers, craftspeople, hunters, gatherers, poets, dancers, musicians, warriors, and kings. For example, black men helped build the pyramids as laborers. Yet, they also were administrators in the Egyptian bureaucracy and reigned as some of the mighty pharaohs, as well.

In the eighth century, groups of black Africans crossed the straits of Gibralter and carried Islam into parts of present day Spain, Portugal, and southwestern France. Others remained on the African continent and built powerful Muslim states in Western Africa. Sundiata Keita, who ruled the kingdom of Mali during the first half of the thirteenth century, transformed it into a great empire. A century later, Mansa Musa, the best known ruler of the ancient Sudan, developed Mali into one of the greatest countries of the medieval world.

Askia Mohammed was a strong leader of the powerful Songhai Empire, which reached its peak under his rule. He seized power in Songhai in 1493 and extended the empire to include territory composed of parts of at least seven current West African countries. Muslim youths came from all over the world to study law and medicine at the University of Sankore at Timbuktu in the Songhai state. Great manuscripts, books, and learned men gathered there to make it one of the intellectual centers of the Muslim world. It was in such centers of culture that art, science, and mathematics flourished.

HOW DID AFRICANS FIRST GET TO AMERICA?

It is not widely known, but in some instances, Africans entered the New World, not as slaves, but as explorers. Africans accompanied both the Spanish and the Portuguese as they explored the lands which became Mexico, Peru, the Caribbean, and the interior of North America. Estavanico, a black man, sailed from Spain in 1527 to explore New Mexico and Arizona for the Spanish. He sent messengers back with wooden crosses to indicate his progress. He was killed by the Indians when they thought he must have been an impostor claiming to be the emissary of white men. Still his work helped open up the Southwest for conquest by the Spanish.

Africans also accompanied the French in their explorations of Canada and the conquest of the Mississippi River valley. Around 1790, Jean Baptiste Point du Sable, a French-speaking black man, erected the first building in the place that later became the city of Chicago. But a far greater number of Africans entered the New World as a result of the European slave trade.

HOW DID THE SLAVE TRADE START?

The European slave trade began as early as the fifth century, when the Portuguese first sailed down the African coast. They came to the continent and made arrangements with some Africans to exchange beads, cloth, and gold dust for slaves. This trade in human beings became a dominant form of commerce and played a crucial financial role in the development of emerging African kingdoms.

Europeans did not create slavery in Africa. Slavery was widespread during the earliest known history of Africa and other places, including ancient Greece, the Roman Empire, and ancient Egypt. Long before the development of the European slave trade, Arabs were transporting African slaves and shipping them off to Arabia, Persia, and other Islamic countries. Slaves were primarily used as servants because there were no large farms in those countries upon which to use unpaid labor. Black Africans were also enslaving one another as the result of war and conquest. But it was the European slave trade that took the greatest toll on Africa and her people. Europeans began bringing African slaves to Europe and making servants of them at the end of the fourteenth century. Some justified the slave trade by declaring that transporting the African out of his native country would allow his conversion from heathen to Christian. Within a few years, the slave trade became an acceptable part of European commerce.

But there was not much use for African labor in banks, shipyards, and businesses. By the last half of the fifteenth century, there were already large masses of unemployed Europeans demanding all available work. It was the New World which offered an opportunity to turn the slave trade profitable. America, with its large deposits of natural resources, was where Europeans hoped to exploit the use of slave labor.

When the European countries undertook to develop the New World, they first turned to the native Indians to work as slaves in the mines and in the fields. But the Indians fell ill with European-imported diseases, and could easily escape back to the sanctuary of their own people and settlements.

So the Europeans turned to Africa for slave labor. They forced kidnapped Africans to march hundreds of miles across the continent to be penned up in prisons while they awaited the slave ships to transport them to America. Then

Africans were crowded into the holds of slave ships, stacked like logs, and chained together in such an inhumane manner that many attempted suicide as the only escape. The Africans were fed meager rations of sometimes spoiled food, and were allowed above deck for fresh air and exercise only a few minutes a day. Many did not survive the trip to the Americas, which was called the Middle Passage.

When the Africans arrived in this country, most were put to work on plantations in the Southern colonies cultivating tobacco, rice, sugarcane, and cotton. A monumental event in the history of slavery occurred in 1793, when a man named Eli Whitney invented the cotton gin. This machine separated seeds from newly picked cotton much more efficiently than the seeds could be separated by hand. The invention dramatically increased the amount of cotton that could be processed. Cotton's price per pound dropped, and demand for the product rose. Along with the demand rose the need for more field hands to cultivate many more thousands of acres of cotton. Since the Southern states were providing more than three-quarters of the world's cotton crop, the economy prospered and cotton became king. But there were not enough white men available to clear the fields and drain the swamps to create new, profitable cotton fields. Southern planters began demanding that greater numbers of African slaves be imported, and unpaid black labor became even more valuable as a vital element to the economy of the South.

WHAT KIND OF LIVES DID THE SLAVES LIVE?

There were many slaves who worked as domestics, skilled artisans, and factory workers, even in the North. But in the South, most slaves worked on the plantations. They lived in crudely built shacks with dirt floors. They slept on mattresses stuffed with corn shucks, and lived on a diet of cornmeal, salt pork, and molasses. They began working in the fields when they were as young as six years old, and were working full-time by the age of ten or twelve. Slaves were often managed by overseers who whipped them or used various forms of torture to make them work, keep them in line, and prevent rebellion. They had little religious freedom and little opportunity to secure an education. Often slaves were sold to other plantations away from their husbands, wives, and families.

When slaves felt they could no longer bear such treatment, they sometimes tried to revolt and take their freedom. One who sought to use the weapon of revolt was a man named Gabriel Prosser, who dreamed of creating a black state. In 1800, Prosser planned an attack on the city of Richmond, Virginia. Six miles outside of Richmond, 1,000 slaves gathered with swords and clubs to begin a march on the city. But a violent storm erupted, and Prosser had to postpone the assault. Before he could reassemble his army, the authorities arrested him. He had been betrayed by two other slaves, and was subsequently hung.

WHAT BROUGHT ABOUT SLAVERY'S END?

As early as the end of the Revolutionary War, Northerners began to question the laws which allowed the buying and selling of humans as slaves. A rift gradually developed between the North and the South over the issue of slavery. The Southerners, despite fears of further rebellion and insurrections, still demanded the use of unpaid black labor to maintain their way of life. The more industrialized North did not rely as heavily on slave labor; therefore, Northerners could more easily raise the issue of its abolition.

The Northern antislavery sentiment developed as ministers, editors, and other leaders of public opinion spoke out against the institution. They declared that slavery was contrary to the teachings of God and contrary to the American way of life. They campaigned by writing pamphlets, books, and petitions, and using the spoken word to promote their cause. In 1831, William Lloyd Garrison began publishing the *Liberator*, claiming that the black man was as much entitled to "life, liberty, and the pursuit of happiness" as the white man. For a whole generation he was a force for nonviolent resistance to slavery.

Frederick Douglass was the foremost African American abolitionist. He escaped from slavery as a very young man in 1838 by displaying to those who asked official-looking papers he had borrowed which were stamped with an American eagle. Many mistook these documents as his freeman's papers. As a literate and articulate victim of slavery, Douglass spoke effectively and eloquently against the practice throughout the United States, despite occasional taunts and threats. In 1847, Douglass decided he needed to start talking directly to the black man about slavery, so he started a newspaper he called the *North Star*, which was later renamed *Frederick Douglass' Paper*.

FREDERICK DOUGLASS

Slaves also sought another means of escaping the horrors of slavery by running away on the Underground Railroad. The Underground Railroad was not an actual railroad, but a series of safe houses and hiding places that led across the South to the North and Canada, where slavery had been abolished. These safe houses were barns, cellars, churches, woodsheds, caves, etc., where white and black people, called "conductors," provided escapees with warm clothing, wagons, food, and shelter from slave hunters who sought to return the slaves to captivity. With the help of more than 3,000 members of the Underground Railroad, it is estimated at least 40,000, and perhaps as many as 100,000, slaves escaped to freedom in the decade preceding the Civil War.

Events escalated in 1859 when a man named John Brown developed a plan to attack slaveholders and liberate their slaves. On October 16, he and a band of fewer than fifty men seized the federal arsenal at Harpers Ferry, Virginia, to get enough ammunition to carry on a full-scale attack against Virginia slaveholders. But federal and state troops were alerted and overwhelmed Brown and his men. Even though Brown and most of his followers were executed, his attack encouraged abolitionists in the North and persuaded thousands who had been indifferent to slavery to protest against it. But John Brown's raid also scared slaveholders in the South and made them think that abolitionists would stop at nothing to wipe out slavery. They started arming themselves and drilling as soldiers. Soon free speech and calm, reasoned thinking disappeared. Southern legislatures began to offer rewards for the arrest of abolitionists such as William Lloyd Garrison and Arthur Tappan as well as for some of the conductors on the Underground Railroad. Some Southerners even went so far as to denounce the Declaration of Independence, and demanded that free black and poor white people be enslaved. They also asked for the reopening of the African slave trade, which had been prohibited by Congress in 1807. They became resolved to destroy every vestige of thought that was against the institution of slavery, even if by force.

By the time newly elected Abraham Lincoln arrived in Washington in March 1861 to assume the role of president, seven states in the South had seceded (withdrawn) from the Union and formed the Confederate States of America. The remaining eight were threatening to leave. In the spring of

JOHN BROWN

1861, a newly formed Southern army attacked Fort Sumter, and the Civil War began.

The average soldier, it seems, did not own slaves; neither did he consider himself an abolitionist. Most Northern soldiers claimed they were fighting to preserve the Union. Most Southern soldiers said they were fighting to preserve what they called "states' rights" or the rights of states to govern themselves. There were many other economic and political reasons for the war, but slavery was the Civil War's single most important provocation. Many slaves fled the South to join the Union armies. But black men and women were only offered a limited role in the war for the first three years. Later, Union forces realized what a valuable role former slaves could play as soldiers (though they were placed in segregated units), support workers, spies, and scouts.

From 1861 to 1865, Northerner fought Southerner. Four hundred seventy thousand people were wounded, and over 620,000 people were killed, making the Civil War the most costly American war in terms of lives lost. But the war did eventually settle the issue of slavery. On June 19, 1862, Lincoln signed a bill abolishing slavery in the territories. On July 17, a measure became law which set free all slaves of disloyal masters coming into Union-held territory. And on January 1, 1863, Abraham Lincoln issued the Emancipation Proclamation, which read: "All persons held as slaves within any State, or designated part of the State, the people whereof shall be in rebellion against the United States, shall be then, thenceforward, and forever free."

HOW DID BLACK PEOPLE LIVE AFTER THE CIVIL WAR?

In 1865, the Confederacy surrendered and the Civil War ended. In December of 1865, the Thirteenth Amendment was ratified and black people, at last, had achieved freedom. But the amendment did not pave the way to a flawless Reconstruction (rebuilding) and reconciliation between the two warring parties. The great disparity between North and South became even more extreme. The Northern industrial financial base grew and prospered during the war, while the South's farm economy, as well as much of the land, had been destroyed. One of the greatest goals of Reconstruction was to rebuild the war-torn South by building a free labor–based economy. But many of the farms disappeared when Southern farmers simply walked away from their failing land. Large plantations had been broken up into small plots, where owners rented out land and housing, and issued credit at the local general store to former slaves in return for part of a crop. Usually these "sharecroppers," as they were called, owed so much money to the general store after the harvest that they were only further in debt by the end of the year.

From 1865 through 1872, a Freedman's Bureau was created by Congress to act as the middleman between the freedman and his ex-master. The Freedman's Bureau gave medical aid, built hospitals, established banks, and distributed food to the freed slaves, who were now virtually destitute. The bureau established schools and helped found practically all the major black colleges. The creation of the Freedman's Bureau was necessary because no laws or other organizations were working toward the goals of helping former slaves. No organization was reuniting families separated by the whims of former slave owners. No other government body was working to create financial independence for these men and women who had, by no choice of their own, been so dependent on others for so long.

Shortly after the Civil War, between 1867 and 1877, African Americans, for the first time, had hopes that they could play an equal role in American society. For the first time, the black man was eligible to vote in every state in the Union. In some Southern states, there were more black than white voters, which propelled African Americans into public office. For the first time, during Reconstruction, there were African Americans in Southern legislatures, making laws that governed white people and black.

Many Southern white men sought to overturn these black-participant governments. Editorial pages in newspapers charged black officeholders with corruption, gross negligence, and incompetence. The white population began to arm itself, and began to search the homes of black people to take away their guns. White people began to make voting more difficult for black people by relocating polling places to isolated sites and revealing their location only to white voters. They also changed the hours of voting to make them unreasonably early, and then closed the polls when African Americans arrived. They also tried intimidation. In 1867, the Ku Klux Klan was born. The Ku Klux Klan was an organization of white men who wore hoods to conceal their identities so that they could whip, maim, terrorize, and even kill African Americans until those who remained submitted to their intimidation. Also, Southerners in Congress were demanding the right to deal with the "Negro problem" in their own way. This meant "home rule," or a suspension of the constitutional safeguards which protected African Americans, to which Congress agreed.

The result was a rule of conduct nicknamed "Jim Crow," in which black people were segregated from members of the white race. This policy began in Tennessee in 1881, but became a way of life in the South and even in other parts of the United States by 1901. It meant that white and black people could not eat in the same restaurants, go to school in the same buildings, use the same rest rooms, or even drink from the same water fountains. The Supreme Court did not uphold the rights of African Americans, but instead, in 1896, in the case of *Plessy v. Ferguson*, held that "separate but equal" facilities for black people were reasonable and not against the law, even though these facilities were hardly "equal."

With the *Plessy* decision came other abridgements of the rights of African Americans. The Southern states began to pile on law after law which separated the races in hospitals, public transportation, funeral homes, prisons, cemeteries, and even asylums.

In the North, the worst of the restrictions meant that black people could not join the trade unions, which denied them the ability to get well-paying jobs. They also could not choose to live in any neighborhood they liked and often had to live in the "colored" part of town.

But in the South, the rules were much more extensive and were written into law. Authorities began establishing arbitrary rules such as poll taxes and literacy tests that were designed to exclude African Americans from voting. And when African Americans tried to challenge these laws, they were, at the least, harassed or jailed, and at the worst, lynched.

It was a difficult period for any African American leader to step forward to challenge this unfair system. But one leader who received a great deal of white as well as black support was Booker T. Washington. Washington denounced social and political inequality but felt that progress would slowly come to black people if they kept quiet and did not protest. He felt they should concentrate on learning a trade, similar to those trades taught at his own Tuskegee Institute. He was opposed to any kind of academic training.

There was disagreement among the black intellectuals about Washington's beliefs. One man in particular, W. E. B.

BOOKER T. WASHINGTON

Du Bois, the author of *The Souls of Black Folk*, led the forces opposing Booker T. Washington's program of conciliation. Du Bois favored immediate social and political integration by direct militant action. He organized black intellectuals and professionals into a protest group, the Niagara Movement, and demanded the abolition of all distinctions based on race and color. The Niagara Movement laid the foundation for the formation of the National Association for the Advancement of Colored People (the NAACP), which still exists as a viable and powerful institution today.

1915 saw the beginning of what was called the Great Migration as hundreds of thousands of black people left the restrictive economic and social conditions of the South to open up the West to settlement and to find jobs in the defense industries in the North and Midwest. During the First World War, thousands of African Americans found jobs in factories, while thousands more entered the army. Despite the fact that black Americans were losing their lives fighting for the freedom of others on foreign shores during World War I, their rights as citizens of this country were still being restricted at home.

W.E.B. Du Bois

The 1920s saw the birth of the "Negro Renaissance." This was a period of exceptional creativity by African American artists, which for the first time allowed even white audiences to appreciate black cultural achievement. Langston Hughes, Countee Cullen, Claude McKay, James Weldon Johnson, Zora Neale Hurston, Duke Ellington, and Bessie Smith were some of the stars of the period. But then the Great Depression, which began in 1929, brought an end to what might be considered the prosperity of the era. As American business went bad, black people became the first employees to lose their jobs.

African American organizations, including the National Urban League, black churches, and newspapers began to

DEPRESSION ERA SOUP LINE

ask for fair play for black people in industries, the armed forces, and government apprenticeship programs. In 1941 A. Philip Randolph organized a march on Washington, D.C., demanding President Franklin D. Roosevelt issue an executive order barring discrimination in war industries and the armed services. Roosevelt finally complied.

During this time, the NAACP was also seeking a way to make a direct attack on segregation. Thurgood Marshall, one of its attorneys, began to challenge state laws which required "separate but equal" facilities for black and white schoolchildren.

THURGOOD MARSHALL

In 1954, the Supreme Court ordered public school desegregation "with all deliberate speed." Despite the ruling of the highest court in the land, there were school districts, including those of Mansfield, Texas, and Little Rock, Arkansas, and the University of Alabama, which tried to prevent black students from enrolling, sometimes even preventing the students from coming in the doors.

WHAT EVENTS MARKED THE BEGINNING OF THE CIVIL RIGHTS MOVEMENT?

ROSA PARKS

In 1955, a seamstress named Rosa Parks was asked by a white bus driver to give up her seat to a white man. When she refused she was arrested. In 1956, other black people in Montgomery, Alabama, began the tactic of the boycott. They refused to ride the city bus lines to avoid being abused by the white drivers. (Among the African Americans leading the Montgomery protest was a young minister named Martin Luther King, Jr.) In 1960, four students from the North Carolina Agricultural and Technical College in Greensboro sat down at a whites-only lunch counter and asked to be served coffee. When they were refused, they sat at the lunch counter until it closed. These and other events began what was called the Civil Rights movement. While some civil rights demonstrations ended peacefully, many, many more ended in violence. Nonviolent protesters across the South were fire-hosed, chased by dogs, and even jailed by the local officials and police. Some lost their lives: four little girls in a Birmingham, Alabama, church were killed by a bomb thrown by a racist extremist.

POLICE DOGS ATTACKING PROTESTORS

The Civil Rights movement marked the beginning of the most fundamental change in black-white relations since the Emancipation Proclamation. Leaders such as Martin Luther King, Jr., and organizations such as the Southern Christian Leadership Conference and the Student Nonviolent Coordinating Committee began to make use of nonviolent methods to help break down the barriers which kept black people as second-class citizens. They planned peaceful demonstrations both in the North and the South to increase job opportunities and to end segregation in housing and education. They supported the African Americans who began to run for office, some of whom were eventually elected to local, state, and national offices for the first time since Reconstruction. Through laws they helped get passed, they attempted to integrate the schools, the armed forces, the government, and virtually every facet of American life.

During the 1960s, another revolution in American society began to evolve as a result of the Civil Rights movement. Women, Hispanic Americans, and other segments of the American population began to look at the gains achieved by African Americans and to ask for an equal place in this society. America's deepening involvement in the Vietnam conflict also caused social upheaval. For the first time in this nation's history, large segments of draft-eligible young men were leaving the country or going to jail to avoid being drafted to fight in a war in whose cause they did not believe. Large protest marches and demonstrations resulted. This was a time of great turbulence in this country.

There was an upheaval of a different kind in the African American community. Black people began to look at themselves differently. Up until this time, they had been calling themselves "Negro" or "colored." They renamed themselves "black" and declared that "Black is beautiful." They formed militant organizations such as the Black Panthers and the Black Muslims and demanded "Black Power." They began to reach back to Africa for their cultural identity. They wore their hair in natural, unstraightened styles. They wore African-style clothing, and renamed themselves or their children with African names. Many Americans began to study African history and African languages, particularly Kiswahili.

HOW DOES KWANZAA FIT INTO THIS?

This was the period of time during which Dr. Maulana Karenga created the holiday of Kwanzaa. Dr. Karenga had long felt that one of the ways to improve the lives of black people in this country was to revive some of the original African values that could enrich African American culture.

Since the 1960s, black people have achieved a great deal politically and economically. African Americans have attained some of the highest ranks in the armed services, such as General Colin Powell, the former chairman of the Joint Chiefs of Staff. African American astronauts, including Mae C. Jemison, Guion S. Bluford, Jr., and the late Ronald McNair have been propelled into space. We have seen the creation of African American millionaires who have achieved their success as businessmen and -women, artists, athletes, and performers. African Americans graduate from major universities in growing numbers, and teach all races at these same universities. African Americans are the mayors of major cities, and black men and women hold seats in the United States Congress and in the president's cabinet. An African American, Jesse Jackson, even ran for president in our recent past. All of these accomplishments were virtually impossible to even imagine just forty years ago.

But forty years ago, it would have been equally hard to imagine how some black neighborhoods have been decimated by the use and sale of illegal drugs, the breakdown of the two-parent family, unemployment, and gang violence. In this time of increased opportunities for all of America's citizens, young black men and women are dropping out of school, dying senselessly in overwhelming numbers, or being jailed as the result of foolish violent acts.

This chapter has noted how black people have struggled from that day over 400 years ago when the first African stepped off a slave ship in America. African Americans are finally achieving equality, by law if not necessarily by practice, but we are now watching as many of these achievements are eradicated by destructive behaviors.

Dr. Karenga's goals for Kwanzaa are more necessary now than ever. By remembering the lessons taught to us by those who came before us, perhaps we can achieve better lives for ourselves and those who will come after us. By practicing the principles of Kwanzaa, all of us, even the children, have the means to make this world a better place.

CHAPTER TWO

WHAT ARE THE SEVEN PRINCIPLES OF KWANZAA AND HOW ARE THEY PRACTICED?

If you place your feet in the footsteps of a great person, you may sometimes trip, but you will never go the wrong way.

—Proverb

You have just read a brief history of Africans and African Americans and learned how their struggle has produced many heroes and heroines. Many people struggled so that you and I can eat in the restaurants of our choice, sit in any seat on the bus we choose, and perhaps even own the bus company *and* the restaurant. Virtually all Americans can now make some significant choices in how they live their lives.

The heroes and heroines that have gone before us have achieved many of their goals by practicing some or all of the principles Dr. Karenga called the Nguzo Saba. By studying these principles, perhaps we can become heroes and heroines in our own way.

WHAT ARE THE PRINCIPLES OF THE NGUZO SABA?

The seven principles of Kwanzaa are:

1. *Umoja* (oo-MOH-jah) or unity—to strive for unity in family, community, nation, and race.
2. *Kujichagulia* (koo-jee-chah-goo-LEE-ah) or self-determination—to speak for ourselves and create our own destinies. To be responsible for ourselves.
3. *Ujima* (oo-JEE-mah) or collective work and responsibility —to build and maintain our community together.
4. *Ujamaa* (oo-jah-MAH) or collective economics—to build and maintain our own stores and businesses.
5. *Nia* (NEE-ah) or purpose—to restore our people to their traditional greatness.
6. *Kuumba* (koo-OOM-bah) or creativity—to use our imagination and creativity to make our community better than when we inherited it.
7. *Imani* (ee-MAH-nee) or faith—to believe in our people, our parents, our teachers, our leaders, and the righteousness of our struggle.

All of these principles may sound hard for a child to follow. How can an eight-year-old build stores or develop communities? These are not goals easily achieved even by adults. The rest of this chapter will tell the stories of how some very special African and African American adults have practiced the principles called the Nguzo Saba. We can learn from their examples.

MARTIN LUTHER KING, JR.

OSEI TUTU

WHO ARE THE HEROES
WHO PRACTICED UMOJA?

Most of us think of Martin Luther King, Jr., and his work when we think of Umoja or unity. Dr. King spent, as well as gave, his life in an effort to unite black people in a non-violent battle to achieve equal rights during the 1950s and 1960s. But we should not ignore those who lived before and after Dr. King who sought to achieve Umoja within their own communities.

Hundreds of years ago a man named Osei Tutu became the first king of the West African kingdom that became Ghana. Under his leadership, a coalition of various chiefs was formed which, for the first time, celebrated a common throne. During his reign, Osei Tutu's kingdom tripled in size. It became a significant power that would endure for two centuries.

Nelson Mandela is another African leader who helped his people achieve unity. As a young lawyer, Mandela sought to free the people of South Africa from the heavily restrictive, discriminatory policies of apartheid, or racial separation. Mandela spent twenty-seven years in jail as a political prisoner because of his beliefs and work. He was finally released from prison on February 12, 1990, and emerged as one of the few black Africans able to persuade the white power struc-

NELSON MANDELA

ture to loosen, and eventually eliminate, apartheid. He later ran for president and succeeded in unifying enough of the black, white, and mixed-race people of South Africa to be elected president of the country in 1994.

WHO WERE THE HEROES AND HEROINES WHO PRACTICED KUJICHAGULIA?

The second principle, Kujichagulia, is the principle of self-determination. Self-determination is when the individual does not allow anyone but him- or herself decide how to live his or her life. This is not about a child simply refusing to listen to a parent or teacher. Self-determination occurs when a person decides to follow a path in life of his or her own choosing.

HARRIET TUBMAN

In the 1800s, during the era of slavery, there were many slaves who risked their lives to escape to freedom. One of the best known was Harriet Tubman, who was born in 1820 and lived until 1913. In 1849, she decided to put her destiny in her own hands by making her escape out of slavery. She then returned to the South nineteen times to help over 300 other slaves escape to freedom. She was never caught and, she once said, she "never lost a passenger." During the Civil War, Harriet Tubman even went behind Confederate lines to spy for the Union.

MALCOLM X

Another black American who sought to determine his own destiny, as well as the destiny of his entire race, was Malcolm X. Born Malcolm Little in 1925 in Omaha, Nebraska, he was forced, when he was still very young, to flee with his family to Lansing, Michigan, to evade white terrorists. Malcolm's father was murdered when the child was six because he would not submit to racist restrictions in that community. Without the benefit of his father's guidance, Malcolm dropped out of school after the eighth grade to live the life of a hustler, drug dealer, and user of drugs. He was sent to prison in 1946, and there he converted to Islam. He became a member of the Nation of Islam, which is also commonly known as the Black Muslims, a religious group which aggressively denounces racism against African Americans. The leader of this Muslim sect, Elijah Muhammad, gave Malcolm the new surname of "X" to replace Little, his "slave name" (a surname derived from an ancestor's slave master). Malcolm X became the most effective and influential spokesman for the Nation of Islam by organizing the temples and increasing the memberships.

But again, Malcolm X sought to determine his own destiny. He left the Nation of Islam in March 1964 and formed his own Muslim Mosque. He converted to Orthodox Islam, changed his name to El-Hajj Malik El-Shabazz, renounced Elijah Muhammad and his teachings, and embraced a more humanistic and global view of relations between the races. After a series of threats, Malcolm X was shot and killed as he spoke to his followers at the Audubon Ballroom in New York City on February 21, 1965. Malcolm X gave his life for freedom, and is not only an example of Kujichagulia, but of Nia (purpose) as well.

Ida B. Wells-Barnett was born in 1862 in Mississippi to slave parents. She attended Fisk University in Nashville, Tennessee, for a year, but began teaching school in the rural South when she was only fourteen years old. However, she was fired when she began protesting the conditions in the black schools. In 1892, Ida Wells began her practice of Kujichagulia when she bought, in part, the *Memphis Free Speech*, a black newspaper, and began to write vigorously about the lynching of black men. In that same year, a white mob destroyed the newspaper's offices and ran Wells out of town.

IDA B. WELLS-BARNETT

Ida Wells settled in Chicago and became associated with the *Chicago Conservator*, whose editor, Ferdinand Lee Barnett, she later married. She also contributed to the founding of the Niagara Movement, the forerunner to the NAACP. She died in Chicago in 1931.

WHO PRACTICED UJIMA?

Ujima, the third principle of Kwanzaa, describes collective work and responsibility for building and creating a better community. Earlier in this century, Ralph Bunche, the grandson of slaves, provided an extraordinary example of Ujima in his life's work to create a better world community. Dr. Bunche helped lay the groundwork for the formation of the United Nations, the worldwide organization that was created as a forum to maintain world peace after the intense devastation of World War II.

RALPH BUNCHE

Dr. Bunche served in the United Nations from 1946 to 1971, working on the Committee on Palestine, acting as a mediator during conflicts between Arabs and Israelis, and bringing about a truce between those nations in 1949. Because of his valiant efforts, Dr. Bunche won the Nobel Peace Prize in 1950.

Medgar Evers also took responsibility to his community very seriously. Evers was a native of Decatur, Mississippi, who fought for America in Europe during World War II. When he returned to this country, he worked vigorously, and under constant threat to his own life, as the field secretary of the Mississippi NAACP. Evers investigated numerous lynchings of black men in Mississippi. He also led efforts to desegregate public facilities in Jackson and the University of Mississippi.

MEDGAR EVERS

Evers knew the work he did was dangerous, and even foretold his own assassination (which occurred in 1963). But it was his sense of Ujima which guided his thoughts and actions, and made him a hero to youth, even today.

WHAT ARE THE SEVEN PRINCIPLES OF KWANZAA?

. . . .

WHO PRACTICED UJAMAA?

The fourth principle, Ujamaa, describes cooperative economics, which is a call to open and maintain black shops and businesses.

During the course of history, black people have often been denied the opportunity to live the American ideal of "the good life" because they have been unable to get well-paying jobs or establish their own businesses. When people have the opportunity to gather funds through savings from work or loans, they can sometimes use those monies to establish their own businesses. A black store owner or serviceperson can prosper if other black people make a conscious effort to buy from those businesses, as opposed to businesses based or owned outside of the community. If the neighborhood business prospers, perhaps the owner will hire local employees. When more people work, more of the income stays in the community to maintain neighborhood institutions. When more people work, a greater sense of pride, self-reliance, and commitment results, and the whole community prospers.

BIDDY MASON

When you think of Ujamaa, or cooperative economics, think of the slave Biddy Mason. Mrs. Mason, at age thirty-two, had to trudge on foot from Mississippi to California as she herded the cattle behind the 300 wagons of her master's caravan. When, in 1856, her master decided to return to Mississippi with his slaves, Mrs. Mason sued in court and convinced the judge that she and her three daughters deserved their freedom. She settled in California and, through her shrewd investments and hard work as a nurse and midwife, she was able to acquire large parcels of land in Los Angeles. She was such a generous person that she even kept an open account at a general store to pay for the purchases of those too poor to pay for their own. She also donated large sums of money to build schools, churches, and nursing homes for black people, some of which still stand today.

A. Philip Randolph, born in Florida in 1889, was another example of a hero who practiced co-operative economics. He organized the first black trade union, the Brotherhood of Sleeping Car Porters and Maids, in 1925, which helped to create better job conditions and higher wages for those who cleaned and carried baggage on the railroads. Mr. Randolph was extremely effective in devising political tactics such as demonstrations, boycotts, and picketing to struggle against discrimination. He once persuaded President Roosevelt to issue an executive order forbidding racial discrimination by threatening a march of 100,000 people on Washington.

A. PHILIP RANDOLPH

A recent example of someone who promotes Ujamaa is the Reverend Jesse Jackson, who was twice a candidate for president of the United States (in 1984 and 1988). Reverend Jackson created an organization called Operation PUSH whose aim was to encourage investment by the major American business corporations in the inner cities. Because of Reverend Jackson's efforts, numerous corporations have provided jobs to black people and sought to support black businesses.

JESSE JACKSON

WHAT IS NIA, AND WHO PRACTICED THAT PRINCIPLE?

Nia, or purpose, is the fifth principle, and its goal is to restore black people to their traditional greatness. Mary McLeod Bethune once said:

MARY McLEOD BETHUNE

We, as African Americans, must recognize that we are the custodians as well as heirs of a great civilization. We have given something to the world as a race and for this we are proud and fully conscious of our place in the total picture of [humankind's] development.

Mary McLeod Bethune was born in 1875 in South Carolina, the youngest of fifteen children. She was committed to improving the lives of young people through education and government service. She founded the Daytona Beach Normal and Industrial School for Negro Girls in 1904, which later became the Bethune-Cookman College. This school became one of the greatest black institutions of higher learning.

Colin Powell is another person who encourages the practice of Nia. He was born in 1937 in New York City to Jamaican immigrant parents. The Powells instilled in their children an appreciation of their West Indian heritage and encouraged them to work hard for their financial security and independence. Young Colin Powell enrolled in college as an engineering major, but floundered a bit, never feeling that engineering was a field in which he could excel. But he became immediately attracted to the Reserve Officers' Training Corps (ROTC) because he felt the training they offered him while still in college prepared him for a career in which he could do well. He graduated, joined the army as a second lieutenant, and won both a Bronze Star and a Purple Heart in the Vietnam War. While he served in the army, his rank steadily rose until he became a general, and ultimately the chairman of the Joint Chiefs of Staff. He directed the United States invasion of Panama in 1989 as well as the successful defeat of the Iraqi forces in the Gulf War in 1991.

COLIN POWELL

He stands as one of the most popular leaders in America of any color and offers himself as a role model for youths by encouraging them to work toward excellence in their own lives, as his parents once encouraged him.

WHAT IS KUUMBA?

The sixth principle, Kuumba, describes creativity in doing what we can to beautify our community and to create a better life for all people. Ever since Africans have been in America they have contributed to the beauty of this nation. There are today hundreds of African Americans who display tremendous talents in music, dance, writing, art, and the theater. And while we may be enchanted with the abilities of modern artists, we should, at Kwanzaa time, remember the pioneers who created such brilliant art years ago, when being a black artist was a very difficult goal.

PHYLLIS WHEATLEY

Remember Phyllis Wheatley, who was born in 1753, and came to this country as a child from Africa. A tailor named Wheatley bought her as a slave and took her home to his wife, where she was taught to read and write. Ms. Wheatley began to write poetry in her teens, and in 1773 became the first black woman to have her work published in America.

Henry Ossawa Tanner was a painter born in Pittsburgh in 1859. Despite his recognition as a master artist, Mr. Tanner found his widest recognition in Europe rather than in his native country because of racial discrimination. Some of his paintings still hang in major museums throughout America and Europe today.

HENRY OSSAWA TANNER

Paul Robeson, born in 1898, exemplified the principle of Kuumba as a celebrated actor, orator, and singer. But he also worked to ease the struggle of the black and white

WHAT ARE THE SEVEN PRINCIPLES OF KWANZAA?

working class in America and for the liberation of the colonized people in Africa.

And Harry Belafonte, born in 1927, is a successful singer, motion picture director, and actor. But he should also be commended for his work as an activist that began with his support of the work of Martin Luther King, as well as his current involvement with human rights issues. Mr. Belafonte exemplifies the qualities of Nia, Ujima, and Kujichagulia, as well as Kuumba.

PAUL ROBESON

HARRY BELAFONTE

WHO PRACTICED THE LAST PRINCIPLE, IMANI?

The seventh principle—Imani—details faith and belief in parents, teachers, and leaders.

Barbara Jordan is one such leader worth following. In 1972, Ms. Jordan became the first black woman ever elected to represent a state from the Deep South in the United States House of Representatives. She made her most stunning impression to the nation and the world when she spoke at the impeachment hearings of President Richard Nixon, as a member of the House Judiciary Committee.

Ms. Jordan, after leaving a renowned and accomplished career in the United States Congress to become a professor at the University of Texas in Austin, had this to say to young people:

> I am telling the young people that if you're dissatisfied . . . with the way things are, then you have got to resolve to change them. . . . It is a burden of black people that we have to do more than talk. We have somehow got to sacrifice our

lives as an example to move young people along so that they will understand that it is a long, slow, tough road to really make it so that it lasts. I have got to offer myself as a role model to others so that perhaps something in my life will help move a young black person who might otherwise drop out to stay in school. That is part of my mission.

BARBARA JORDAN

A final example of a figure who practiced Imani, as well as the other six principles of the Nguzo Saba, is Dr. Martin Luther King, Jr., the African American hero mentioned first in this chapter. Dr. King was an extraordinary man who left an extraordinary legacy in his successful protest against racial inequity in America, for which he is still honored years after his death. Dr. King learned many lessons from those who lived before him, and found a way to utilize those teachings to improve the quality of life for all of the world's citizens.

When he was a seminary student, Martin Luther King, Jr., studied the works of Mahatma Gandhi, who sought to free the Indian people from the oppression of colonial rule. Gandhi's philosophy was that all protest against the British would be more effective if it was nonviolent and peaceful. Dr. King put into practice this idea of peaceful resistance and led the nonviolent Civil Rights movement that began in the mid-1950s until his death in 1968.

MARTIN LUTHER KING, JR.

His civil rights work also reinforced the principles of Kujichagulia (self-determination), Ujamaa (cooperative economics), and Ujima (collective work and responsibility). Because of the rights fought for by Dr. King during the 1950s and 1960s, many black Americans were finally allowed the opportunity to further their educations, acquire good jobs, buy and operate their own businesses, own their own homes in a wider range of neighborhoods, and generally improve the quality of life for themselves and their children.

Dr. King used Kuumba to create a better life for all people, Umoja to unify black people, and Nia when he worked to restore black people to their traditional greatness. Dr. King once said, "If you will protest courageously, and yet with dignity and Christian love, when history books are written in future generations, the historians will have to pause and say, 'There lived a great people—a black people—who injected new meaning and dignity into the veins of civilization.' This is our challenge and our overwhelming responsibility."

CHAPTER THREE

WHAT ARE THE SYMBOLS OF KWANZAA AND HOW ARE THEY USED IN THE CELEBRATION?

No matter how high a house is built, it must stand on something.

—Proverb

Now that we've learned what the Seven Principles of Kwanzaa, or the Nguzo Saba, are, we need to discover what the seven symbols of Kwanzaa represent and how they are used.

The seven symbols of Kwanzaa are:

1. *Mkeka* (m-KAY-kah)—the mat, which is the symbol of tradition and the foundation on which all the other symbols rest.
2. *Mazao* (mah-ZAH-oh)—the crops, which are the result of the harvest and represent productive labor.
3. *Kinara* (kee-NAH-rah)—the candleholder, which represents the African ancestors.
4. *Muhindi* (moo-HEEN-dee)—the corn, which represents children and the future. (Also referred to as *Vibunzi,* which means one ear of corn.)
5. *Zawadi* (zah-WAH-dee)—gifts given as an act of sharing and a labor of love.

6. *Kikombe cha Umoja* (kee-KOHM-bay chah oo-MOH-jah)—the unity cup, which represents family and community unity.
7. *Mishumaa Saba* (mee-shoo-MAH SAH-ba)—the seven candles, which represent the Seven Principles of the Nguzo Saba.

Two supplementary symbols are the *Bendera ya Taifa* (bayn-DAY-rah yah tah-EE-fah), which is the African American unity flag, and a poster featuring the Seven Principles.

HOW ARE THESE SYMBOLS USED DURING KWANZAA?

Kwanzaa is a relatively new festival, and your family or organization can exhibit great creativity or Kuumba in how it is observed. The area of your home where Kwanzaa will be observed can be decorated with the same skill and creativity that is used in decorating for Christmas or other holidays, like Halloween, or special occasions. Banners and posters can be created or the poster found on page 35 can be enlarged on a photocopy machine and then colored. Sculptures and other African-influenced artwork can be created or gathered to enhance the area around the Kwanzaa table.

You and your family can use a great deal of creativity in how you observe the festival. The members of your organization or your family can dress partially or fully in African clothing. They can consider the ceremony cultural while they simply recite the proverbs found at the beginning of each chapter of this book, or they can make the observances more spiritual and recite prayers.

The Kwanzaa table should first be covered with a black or green tablecloth, upon which the Mkeka (straw mat) is placed. The Kinara (candleholder) holding the Mishumaa Saba (seven candles) is next placed in the center of the Mkeka. A black candle is placed in the center of the Kinara, three red candles are placed on the left, and three green candles are placed on the right. The symbols for the Mazao, which are fruit and vegetables, are next placed in a basket on the table to symbolize the prosperity of the harvest. Ears of corn (Muhindi), which can be Indian corn, are placed on the table to symbolize the children in the family. An ear of corn (Vibunzi) should be placed on the Mkeka for each child; however, if there are no children in the family, at least one ear should be placed on the Mkeka as a symbol of all the children in the community. Books that symbolize the Zawadi, or heritage symbols like African sculpture or handmade crafts of African origin, should be placed in the Kwanzaa setting to balance and enhance the table. For wall decorations, you can hang a Nguzo Saba poster, or the Bendera ya Taifa, which is the black, red, and green flag conceived by Marcus Garvey. He was an activist who created the first nationalist movement among African Americans. The black is for the people, the red is for the continuing struggle, and the green is for the future.

THE FIRST DAY OF KWANZAA— DECEMBER 26

On each day of Kwanzaa, a member of the family lights a candle. Traditionally this family member is a child. On December 26, the first day of Kwanzaa, the boy or girl lights the black candle to represent the first principle of Nguzo Saba, which is Umoja. Then the child makes a brief statement about the first principle. The statement could be as simple as, "The first principle of Kwanzaa is Umoja or unity. I hope we will always stay together as a strong and loving family." The eldest member of the family might, at this time, discuss the principle of Umoja a little further by telling what the principle means to him or her, or by reading from a passage that explains the principle in more detail. Then the members of the family, from oldest down to the youngest, can take a drink of fruit juice from the Kikombe cha Umoja (unity cup). Or if it is the family's preference, the unity cup can simply be left to sit at the center of the table holding a small symbolic amount of wine or juice. Every member of the family can drink from his or her own cup. Then the candle can be blown out for the next day's observances.

THE SECOND DAY—DECEMBER 27

On the second day a child again lights the black candle, and then lights the farthest red candle on the left for the second principle of the Nguzo Saba. The child can say something like, "The second principle of Kwanzaa is Kujichagulia, or self-determination. I will do all that I can to study and get good grades in school because I know that my future is up to me." An adult might also discuss self-determination. The whole family drinks from the unity cup and the candles are then extinguished.

THE THIRD DAY—DECEMBER 28

On December 28, the third day, the child again lights the black candle, the red candle farthest on the left, and then the green candle farthest on the right. The candles are lit in alternate colors to symbolize the struggle (represented by the red candles) which comes before a safe, clean, healthy world (represented by the green candles) can be achieved. The child can then discuss the third principle of Kwanzaa. He or she might say: "The third principle of Kwanzaa is Ujima or collective work and responsibility. Even though I am a child, I am an important part of my neighborhood and community. I should do whatever I can to make sure it is a safe, clean, and beautiful place to live." After this, an adult might explain the principle of Ujima further. Everyone again drinks from the unity cup, and the candles are extinguished.

THE FOURTH DAY—DECEMBER 29

On this day the family member lighting the candle will light the black candle, the red candle farthest on the left, the green candle farthest on the right, and then the next red candle on the left. The child might then say, "The fourth principle of Kwanzaa is Ujamaa, or collective economics. I should help to make my community strong by doing most of my shopping in my neighborhood." The eldest family member might explain that by shopping in the neighborhood, business will increase in neighborhood stores. If business increases, the store owners may hire more people in the community to work for them. Therefore, more people in the community will have money to spend, and the whole community can prosper.

Again, everyone drinks from the unity cup, and the candles are extinguished.

THE FIFTH DAY—DECEMBER 30

On the fifth day of Kwanzaa, the child will light the candles again in the order of black, red, green, red, and then green, starting from the outside in. She or he might then say, "The fifth principle of Kwanzaa is Nia or purpose. We should all work together to build our community."

Again the eldest member of the family might explain how Nia could be achieved by organizing block clubs, cleaning up a deserted lot, or organizing a group to paint and repair the home of an elderly or disabled neighbor. The family drinks from the unity cup, and then extinguishes the candles.

THE SIXTH DAY—DECEMBER 31

The sixth day of Kwanzaa occurs on December 31, which is New Year's Eve. From this celebration onward, December 31 can be a day of another rich tradition in your family, that of the Kwanzaa *Karamu* or feast. This particular celebration is something special, and is the best day of the holiday to invite friends and other family members over to enjoy the festival. The family can put up additional decorations, wear full African dress, and select African and African American music to enhance the party atmosphere. The most enjoyable part of the celebration is the cooking and eating of a wonderful feast. Guests can also bring various favorite dishes to complement the meal.

Greet guests at the door with *"Habari gani?"* (ha-BAR-ee GON-ee), which means "What's new?" The guests should respond, "Kuumba," which is the sixth principle of Kwanzaa, and the principle for that particular day. Zawadi or gifts can be exchanged among the guests, or simply given by the hosts to the guests. The children and/or adults can do performances of Kwanzaa plays, read poems they have written themselves, or tell uplifting stories. There can also be readings about welcoming guests, remembering the past and those that lived before, reassessing each life and the present, recommitting oneself to improvement, and rejoicing that friends or families are together again. Dr. Karenga discusses these ideas in his book, *The American Holiday of Kwanzaa*, and they are derived directly from the African first fruit festivals. The lighting of the sixth candle then becomes a very beautiful and enjoyable event. The person lighting the candle might say, "This is the sixth day of Kwanzaa, and the principle is Kuumba, or creativity. We have all worked very hard to create a Kwanzaa Karamu that we can all remember with pride." A libation should be poured in remembrance of ancestors. Everyone can then drink from one or several unity cups, and the candles are extinguished.

At the end of the Karamu, everyone stands as the eldest member of the family reads the *Tamshi La Tutaonana* (TAM-shi la Tu-ta-u-NA-na), which Dr. Karenga wrote as a farewell statement for both the feast and the year. It reads:

> Strive for discipline, dedication and achievement in all you do. Dare struggle and sacrifice and gain the strength that comes from this. Build where you are and dare leave a legacy that will last as long as the sun shines and the water flows. Practice daily Umoja, Kujichagulia, Ujima, Ujamaa, Nia, Kuumba and Imani. And may the wisdom of the ancestors always walk with us. May the year's end meet us laughing and stronger. May our children honor us by following our example in love and struggle. And at the end of next year, may we sit again together, in larger numbers, with greater achievement and closer to liberation and a higher level of human life.

Then the elder should lead all the guests in the *Harambee* (ha-RAM-bee) salute. Harambee means "Let's pull together," and the salute is a show of solidarity. Everyone raises his or her right fist about shoulder high, and then pulls down forcefully until the elbow is next to his or her torso, say-ing, "Harambee!" seven times in unison. This concludes the Karamu celebration.

THE SEVENTH DAY—JANUARY 1

The last day of Kwanzaa is January 1. The child should lead the candlelighting ceremony by lighting first the black candle, then alternating from red to green, starting from the outside in until all the candles are lit. The child might then say, "This is the seventh and last day of Kwanzaa. The seventh principle is Imani, or faith. We should all believe in our people—our parents, our teachers, our leaders—and that the struggle we are engaged in is right." An adult can discuss this principle further. Then the family takes one last drink out of the unity cup. All seven candles of Kwanzaa are extinguished for the last time.

This is a very simple outline for a basic Kwanzaa ceremony. Your family can determine if this is the ceremony you would like to observe, or whether you would like to personalize it in any way. For instance, you might want to make the ceremony more spiritual, and add prayers. Or your family might be very small, and you might want to invite different guests, adult and child, every day.

There are other variations you might try. You might alternate the person who lights the candle. It could be one child one day; another child, the next; and then perhaps a parent. The statement of principle made after the candle lighting could be followed by a reading of poetry, a song, a thought for the day, one of the proverbs that heads these chapters, one of the biographies from chapter 2, or a reading that demonstrates the principle. If yours is a storytelling family, perhaps you could tell a story. Or your family might want to show videos of the Kwanzaa festival from the year before.

Your family can exchange books, heritage symbols, or other small, handmade Zawadi (gifts) every day of the celebration or just on December 31. Or you can give a gift to the people in your community and take the Kinara and the other elements of the Kwanzaa table to a local convalescent home or community center so that the ceremony can be shared with many friends. You and your family can create a holiday tradition that can be observed by your family for generations to come.

CHAPTER FOUR

CRAFTS TO MAKE BEFORE KWANZAA

You can't reap what you sow until you've planted the seed.

—Proverb

One of the joys of preparing for Kwanzaa is that most of the articles, implements, and products of the holiday can be made by hand. Kwanzaa promotes the creation of gifts and decorations as a demonstration of love rather than simply buying them. By following the instructions in this book you can learn to make things with simple materials found about the house, easily purchased in crafts or art supply stores, or ordered through catalogs.

Most of the items you will create are easy to make, but adult supervision is recommended for any child under twelve years old. There will, however, be instructions for crafts that can be made by children as young as five.

The crafts will be classified into three levels of ease or difficulty: easy, skilled, and challenge. In this chapter, there are directions on how to make the Kinara, the Mkeka, candles, and other items for the Kwanzaa table. Instructions for many other items to decorate the Kwanzaa table, and items to make as Zawadi, or gifts, are included in chapter 5.

THE KINARA

The Kinara symbolizes all of the generations of Africans that came before us. It is a candleholder that holds seven candles, which represent the Nguzo Saba, the principles which are the heart and soul of Kwanzaa. All of these candleholders should be considered a challenge to make because they must be properly assembled. If the candleholder is made poorly, the lit candles could fall off and create a fire. Have an adult supervise your preparation of these items, and make sure your Kinara is inspected again before the candles are lit.

ITEM: CHILDREN'S BLOCK KINARA

CHALLENGE: *3 hours preparation time over 2 days*

SUPPLIES NEEDED

1 wooden plank (Douglas fir or pine), 1" high by 4" wide by 15" long

Medium-grain sandpaper

Wood glue or glue gun

8 wooden 1 1/2" children's blocks which can spell KWANZAA, leaving the eighth block blank. (Or the last block may be the number of years you have been celebrating Kwanzaa. For example, on your third Kwanzaa you would use the number 3, as above.)

Hammer

8 to 10 finishing nails, 1 1/4" long

Shellac, turpentine, 1 paint brush

7 tapered candles: 3 green, 3 red, 1 black

Butter knife

DIRECTIONS

Sand smooth the rough edges of the wooden plank. Place the blocks spelling KWANZAA evenly spaced on the board,

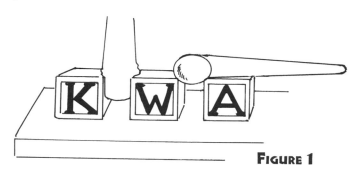

FIGURE 1

leaving approximately 5/8" to 3/4" distance between the blocks, depending on how thick your candle bottoms are. (See Figure 1.) The space should be slightly narrower than the width of the bottom of your candles. Glue all seven

blocks in place on the board with wood glue. Let the glue dry. Turn the board over and nail the blocks in place from the underside. (See Figure 2.) Coat both the blocks and the board with two coats of shellac. Clean your brush with turpentine. Allow the candleholder to dry overnight.

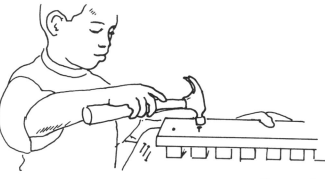

FIGURE 2

Shave two sides of the candles with the butter knife so that the candles just barely fit between the blocks. Insert the candles between the blocks in this order: three green on the right, one black in the center, three red on the left. Make sure the candles fit snugly. The more snug the fit, the less likely the candles will fall over.

ITEM: DRILLED CHILDREN'S BLOCK KINARA

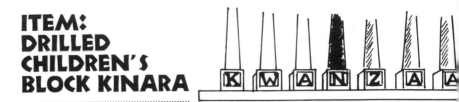

CHALLENGE: *4 hours preparation time over 2 days*

SUPPLIES NEEDED

Same as block Kinara

Additional Supplies Needed: Drill with 1" drill bit

DIRECTIONS

Follow the instructions for preparing the wooden board as for the previous project. This time you will only be using the seven blocks that spell the word KWANZAA. Place the blocks so they are an equal distance apart on the plank. (On a 15"-long plank, using 1 1/2" square blocks, there should be 1/2" space between the blocks and 3/4" space on each end. See Figure 3.) Glue the bottom of the blocks to the wooden board. Allow time to thoroughly dry. Have an adult drill a 1" hole in the top of each block. The hole should be at least 3/4" deep. Turn the board over and nail the blocks to the other side. Place the candles securely in the holes. If the holes are too big, drip candle wax from a burning candle into the holes and insert the candle while the wax is still liquid. If the hole is too small, have an adult drill to make it larger.

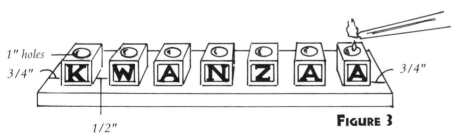

1" holes
3/4"
3/4"
1/2"

FIGURE 3

ITEM: LARGE WOODEN BLOCK KINARA

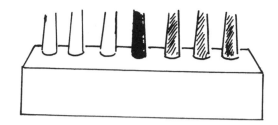

CHALLENGE:
4 hours preparation time over 2 days

SUPPLIES NEEDED

1 large wooden block, 3" high by 3" deep by 15" long

Ruler

Pencil

Drill with 1" drill bit

Sandpaper

Shellac or wood stain

7 tapered candles: 3 red, 3 green, 1 black

DIRECTIONS

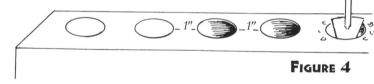

FIGURE 4

Measure off seven circles that are 1" across and 1" apart on the wooden block. There should be a 1" space on each end. (See Figure 4.) Ask an adult to drill 1" holes in the circles you have indicated.

Sand all rough edges, including the block ends and the holes in which the candles sit. Shellac or stain and shellac the wooden block. Allow to dry overnight. Place the candles in the holes in the proper order: three red on the left, three green on the right, and one black in the middle. If the candle does not fit in the hole securely, have an adult help you drip some melted wax into the hole and then insert the candle in the wax while it is still liquid.

ITEM: SCULPTURAL ASSEMBLAGE KINARA

CHALLENGE: *4 hours preparation time over 2 days*

SUPPLIES NEEDED

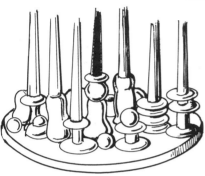

Sandpaper

15" wooden circle made out of plywood or particle board

Woodcraft parts (These can be purchased as a bag of turned, cored wooden accessories in crafts stores, lumber yards, or ordered from crafts catalogs. Some stores even sell small wooden holders for candles.)

Wood glue or glue gun

Shellac

Paintbrush

DIRECTIONS

Sand all rough edges. Assemble the parts on the wooden circle in a creative and artistic way, constructing seven candleholders. Glue the pieces in place. Allow time to dry. Shellac the whole assemblage. Allow 24 hours to dry. Have an adult drip melted wax in all the holders so that the candles sit in them securely.

ADDITIONAL IDEAS

The preceding projects are just a few examples of candle-holders you can construct. If you do not have the time or materials, you might simply take three red votive candles, three green votive candles, and one black votive candle and float them in a pretty decorative bowl filled with water. Or you could just gather seven assorted candleholders holding three red candles, three green candles, and one black candle, and assemble them in an artistic arrangement on the Kwanzaa table. Whatever Kinara you choose to make, use your Kuumba, or creativity, and make sure your construction is safe.

THE MISHUMAA SABA (CANDLES)

The Mishumaa Saba, or seven candles, denote the Nguzo Saba or Seven Principles of Kwanzaa. The candles are placed securely in the Kinara (which represents ancestry) to symbolize how the Seven Principles are rooted in "the way of the ancestors," according to Dr. Karenga.

   I have only included instructions on how to create one kind of candle. Certainly, there are hand-dipped candles you can make or sand candles you can cast, but I have not included directions for those here. Since ready-made candles are widely available and inexpensive, I thought you might want to put your energies to use creating other products that are not so common.

ITEM: BEESWAX CANDLES

EASY: *1 hour preparation time*

SUPPLIES NEEDED

   Sheets of beeswax, in green, red, and black

   Wicks

   Scissors

DIRECTIONS

Cut a 4" x 5" section of beeswax. Cut a length of wick so that it is 1/4" longer than the beeswax. Place the wick at the edge

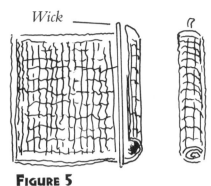

Wick

FIGURE 5

of beeswax, and then roll the beeswax around the wick. (See Figure 5.) If the wax is stiff, bring it close to a heat source like the stove or a heater, and the wax will soften. Securely seal the edge so that the candle will not come apart.

THE MKEKA (MAT)

The Mkeka, which is a typical African item, stands for tradition and history. All the other Kwanzaa items sit on the Mkeka because it is the foundation, similar to the way tradition and history are the foundations for understanding the world around us. The following two projects show you how you can weave your own Mkeka.

WEAVING

In West Africa, it is possible to tell whether a man or a woman wove a piece of cloth by the width of the woven strips. Traditionally, a male weaver will make his living by traveling from village to village carrying a small loom, weaving strips four to six inches wide. A woman weaves larger strips, sometimes up to twenty inches wide, on a bigger loom which is fixed in place in her village or settlement.

The strips of cloth, whether narrow or wide, are then sewn together to create the items of clothing or covering required. The man usually weaves in exchange for food for his family. The woman weaves to clothe herself and her children. According to tradition, it is considered unlucky to begin a new piece of weaving on a Friday.

ITEM: CLOTH MAT

EASY: *2 hours preparation time*

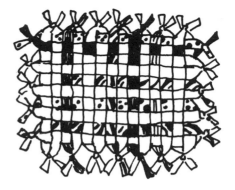

SUPPLIES NEEDED

Strips of cloth, in yellow, white, red, green,
   or black or in bold graphic patterns,
   1/2" wide and 26" long for horizontal
   strips and 1/2" wide and 20" long for
   vertical strips

Sheet of 12" x 18" foamboard

Scissors

Stapler and staples

Staple remover

DIRECTIONS

Lay the longer strips of cloth across
the foamboard lengthwise, alternating colors or patterns, allowing 3" of
the strips to extend past both sides of
the foamboard. Staple the ends down. (See Figure 6.) Inter-
weave the shorter strips of cloth in the vertical direction,
alternating colors, allowing for 3" of fringe. By the time you
finish weaving, the mat should be the approximate size of

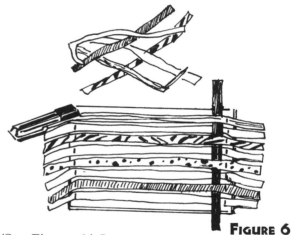

FIGURE 6

the foamboard, not count-
ing the fringe.

   Starting from one corner,
knot pairs of the fringe strips
together until the whole
mat is done. Then release
the staples. (See Figure 7.)

FIGURE 7

ITEM: WOVEN YARN MAT

SKILLED: *15 hours preparation time*

SUPPLIES NEEDED

   1 skein each of 4-ply worsted yarn in green, red, and black, or 3 skeins in a natural color

   1 package of plastic drinking straws

   1 knitting needle

   1 sewing needle with a very large eye (for yarn)

   4 buttons without buttonholes

DIRECTIONS

Cut two straws in half. Measure off four lengths of yarn 30" long from any skein. Push one end of the yarn through the

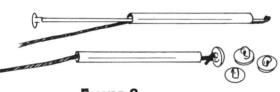

FIGURE 8

straw. You may need a long knitting needle to push the yarn through. Once you have pushed a length of yarn through each of the four straws, tie a button to the end of it so that it cannot slip back through the straw. (See Figure 8.)

Hold the straws in the left hand with the buttoned ends sticking up. Attach the end of yarn from one of the skeins to one of the outside straws about midway up the straw. Then weave the wool in and out across the loom, holding the straws firmly, but not tightly. (See Figure 9.) As you wrap the yarn in and out of the straws, the weaving will

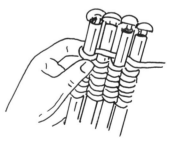

FIGURE 9

gradually work its way down the straw, and onto the yarn, almost by itself. You can make this process a little easier by pulling the straws up and free of the weaving an inch or two at a time. (See Figure 10.)

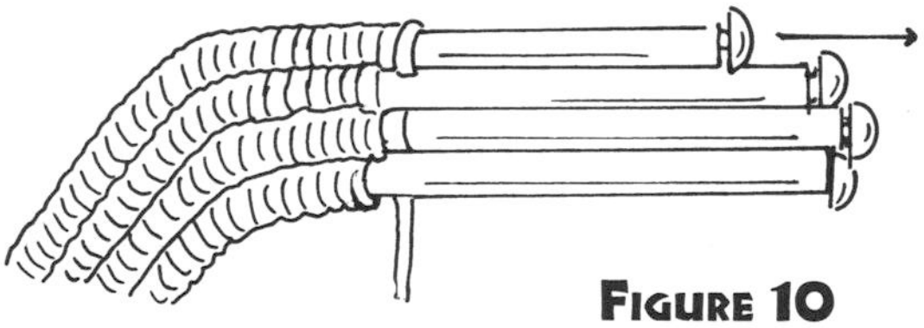

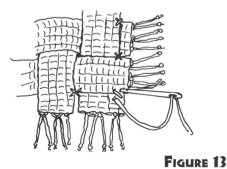

FIGURE 10

Continue weaving until you are within 10" of the end of your yarn. Push all of the weaving off the straws and use your fingers to even out the tension. Cut off the buttons and pull off the four straws. Makc knots at the ends of the fringe and tie pairs of fringe together until you have just two knotted cords at both ends of your woven panel. (See Figure 11.) You may want to add 10" lengths of yarn folded in half to make additional fringe. Make six 30" woven panels like this in the various colors (each panel has 5" of fringe on one end, 20" of weaving, and 5" of fringe on the other end). Make eight more woven panels that are 22" long (each panel has 5" of fringe on one end, 12" of weaving, and 5" of fringe on the other end). Weave together the 30" panels with the 22" panels to make the mat. (See Figure 12.) Thread the needle with a length of one of the colors of yarn. Sew the mat together by making a few stitches where the panels touch on the edge near the fringe. (See Figure 13.)

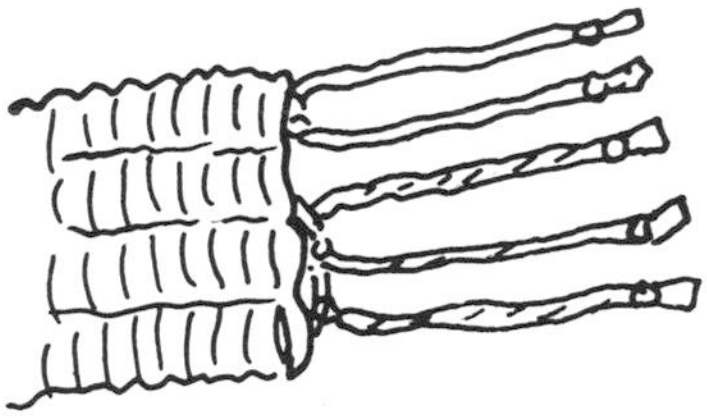

FIGURE 11

FIGURE 12

FIGURE 13

MAZAO BASKET

The Mazao, or crops, reflect the historical roots of the holiday as a celebration of the harvest. They also represent the rewards of collective labor.

It is very easy to find or buy an inexpensive basket to hold the various fruits and vegetables that should be in your Kwanzaa setting. If, however, you would like to try to create your own, the following are instructions on how to make a bowl out of *papier-mâché*.

PAPIER-MÂCHÉ

The use of papier-mâché (from the French meaning chewed-up paper) goes back 2,000 years to China. The craft uses pulped or glued paper to mold forms, a technique still being used today by sculptors, craftsmen, and schoolchildren. Papier-mâché is also popularly used to make carnival and religious masks all over the world. Through this craft, you can create one-of-a-kind works of art that can become part of your family's Kwanzaa tradition for years.

The method I describe can be used to form several of the papier-mâché objects featured in this and the next chapter.

The objects can be as small as a bead or as large as a free-standing sculpture.

The method I recommend involves tearing scrap paper into small strips, slathering the strips with glue, and then layering them over a shape to achieve a form. Some artists prefer not to use newspaper for their sculptures because its acid content sometimes turn the items yellow in time. But you can certainly use it if there is no other scrap paper available. After the papier-mâché dries, you can paint the surface with bright acrylic paints.

While making papier-mâché objects is not particularly hazardous, it can be very messy. Adult supervision is highly recommended throughout the creation of these projects. Cover your work surfaces with newspaper, and wear old clothes when you make these items. The acrylic paint I recommend to decorate your crafts is permanent, and can permanently stain your clothes or your furniture, so use it with care. The colors are very vivid, however, and are perfect to use with a number of crafts. Immediately wipe spilled acrylic paint off surfaces like the floor or worktable. Keep paint-filled brushes in a jar of water when not in use. If the paint dries on the brush, the brush will have to be thrown away.

ITEM: MAZAO BOWL

SKILLED: *4 hours preparation time over 2 days*

SUPPLIES NEEDED

Large plastic bowl, rubber ball, or other large round shape to use as a mold

Plastic bag

Paper towels

Bucket

2-pound package of wallpaper paste powder

Scrap paper torn into strips (like computer paper, brown wrapping paper, or recycled junk mail)

Scissors

Acrylic gesso and paints in assorted colors

Paintbrushes

DIRECTIONS

Cover your working surface with newspapers and yourself with an apron or old clothes. Cover the mold surface with a plastic bag, whether it is the inside of a bowl (See Figure 14) or the outside of a round surface, like a ball, propped up off the table's surface (See Figure 15). Wet a paper towel and lay it on top of the plastic so the papier-mâché will not stick. Mix some of the wallpaper paste powder in the bucket with water until it is the consistency of paste. Coat both sides of the paper strips with paste using your fingers and add the strips on top of the paper towel layer in various directions until the papier-mâché bowl is at least 3/4" thick.

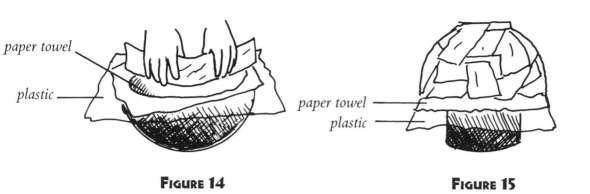

paper towel

plastic

paper towel

plastic

FIGURE 14

FIGURE 15

Make sure the base is flat so the bowl will sit securely on the table. Leave the bowl to dry overnight. Detach it carefully from the plastic. You can use scissors to cut an even edge at the top of the bowl. Coat both sides of the bowl with acrylic gesso. The following are some of the many different ways you can decorate your Mazao bowl with acrylic paint.

THE KIKOMBE CHA UMOJA (UNITY CUP)

The Kikombe cha Umoja, or unity cup, is used nightly in the ritual in which all the members of the family take a drink during the Kwanzaa ceremony. This ritual reinforces the sense of unity within the family and the community.

Sometimes during the Kwanzaa ceremony, a family might wish to honor their ancestors by pouring a "libation" from the unity cup. A libation is usually a few drops of wine or juice poured out on the ground as a symbolic offering. However, your family can simply pour some of the fruit juice or wine from the Kikombe cha Umoja into a bowl set aside for the occasion.

Since the construction of a cup or goblet is more than most children, or even adults, can do easily, I am suggesting that you take an existing wine glass or goblet and decorate it specifically for Kwanzaa. If family members intend to drink from the cup, it would be best if the decorations can be taken off the cup every evening so that it can be washed. Decorations can be as simple as a kente cloth ribbon, a holiday corsage, or a group of red, green, and black strings and tassels wrapped around the stem; or wrap the whole goblet in aluminum foil. Use your Kuumba to create the unity cup, and all the objects with which you decorate your Kwanzaa table.

THE BENDERA YA TAIFA (UNITY FLAG)

Marcus Garvey, the black nationalist, in his promotion of all things black, established the red, black, and green unity flag for African Americans. Dr. Karenga reinterpreted the colors of the flag so that black represented the people, and was to come first, because the people came first. Red, Dr. Karenga advised, was for the struggle by the people for a free and fulfilling life. Green represented the future, for which we must all take responsibility.

The following are instructions for a unity flag that can be hung as a banner on the wall behind your Kwanzaa table.

ITEM: BENDERA YA TAIFA

EASY: *2 hours preparation time*

SUPPLIES NEEDED

1/3 yard of cotton cloth in each of the following colors: black, red, and green

Ruler

Pen

Scissors

Common pins

Red or black spool of thread

Iron

Sewing machine (if available) or sewing needle

DIRECTIONS

Measure off with the ruler and pen two 6" x 24" strips from each color of cloth. The grain or fibers of the cloth should flow in the direction of the 24" length. Cut out the cloth strips you have drawn. Place one black and one red strip, right sides together. Pin the strips along one of the 24" sides. Have an adult sew the pinned sides together on a sewing machine, or carefully sew the pieces together with the needle and thread, allowing a 1/2" seam. (See Figure 16.) Pin one green strip to the unsewn edge of the red strip, right sides together. Sew the pinned sides together allowing for a 1/2" seam. (See Figure 17.) Make sure all sides of the rectangle you have sewn are perfectly straight and all corners are perfectly square.

Make another banner following the instructions above. Pin the two banners, right sides together, and then sew a 1/2" seam all around, leaving a 3" opening on one side. (See Figure 18.) Pull the project inside out and slip stitch the opening closed. (See Figure 19.)

With the addition of the Bendera ya Taifa and the Nguzo Saba poster from page 35 enlarged on a photocopy machine and colored, you now have all the handmade elements to complete your Kwanzaa table.

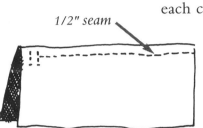

1/2" seam

FIGURE 16

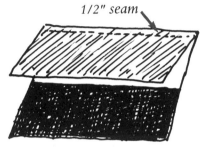

1/2" seam

FIGURE 17

opening

FIGURE 18

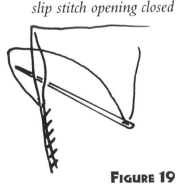

slip stitch opening closed

FIGURE 19

CHAPTER FIVE

GIFTS TO MAKE FOR KWANZAA

To learn to make a thing is better than having the wealth to buy two of those things.

—Proverb

One of the best parts of Kwanzaa preparation is the creation of gifts for family members and friends. Even though Kwanzaa occurs during the traditional Christmas and Hanukkah gift-giving seasons, it goes one step further. It encourages you as a celebrant to produce, with your own hands, gifts to be given as demonstrations of your love. Imagine how satisfying it will be to watch a member of your family open, for example, a musical instrument that you made wrapped in gift wrap that you designed, and played in a musical production that you put together for the Karamu. Making the present can also return tremendous gifts back to the maker—knowledge of how to make the craft and pride in workmanship.

The following are detailed instructions on how to make various items that you can give as gifts. They are, as in the previous chapter, classified as to how difficult or easy they are to produce; however, virtually all of these crafts will require an adult to advise and aid you. Most of the materials needed can be found around the house. But there will be some crafts materials you will have to buy. These materials are inexpensive and available in most art supply, craft, or hardware stores. A list of suppliers is included in chapter 9.

JEWELRY

ITEM: PAPIER MÂCHÉ BRACELET

(see the information in chapter 4 about papier-mâché)

SKILLED: *3 hours preparation time over 2 days*

SUPPLIES NEEDED

Cardboard

Ruler

Scissors

Stapler

Scrap paper cut into 1" strips (about 10)

Small bag of wallpaper paste powder

Bucket

Sandpaper

Acrylic paint

Paintbrushes

DIRECTIONS

Since papier-mâché is fairly messy, make sure the top of your table or working surface is completely covered in newspaper.

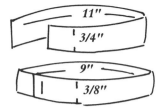

FIGURE 1

If you are making a bracelet for an adult, cut a cardboard strip that is 3/4" wide by 11" long. For a child, cut a strip that is slightly smaller—perhaps 5/8" wide by 9" long. Make a loop by overlapping the two ends of the strip and stapling the ends together. (See Figure 1.) Try the cardboard bracelet on your wrist to make sure the bracelet is big enough to get on and off your wrist easily. Allow a bit of extra room for the additional thickness of the papier-mâché to be added. (See Figure 2.)

FIGURE 2

Add water to 1/2 cup of the wallpaper paste powder in the bucket and mix it with your hand until it is the consistency of a paste. As you mix the paste, it will thicken slightly. Then cover the strips of paper with the paste using your fingers. Wrap the pasted strips around the cardboard loop until you have created a thickness of about 1/4". (See Figure 3.) Smooth the papier-mâché on the hoop so there are no rough ridges or areas on either the inside or the outside of the band. Allow two days for the band to dry. Sand rough spots, if necessary, with sandpaper.

FIGURE 3

Thin the acrylic paints with water in jars to the consistency of a thin milk shake and paint a design on the dry bracelet. See the beginning of these instructions for examples of designs you can use.

Remember, when you use acrylic paints, you should never allow the paint to dry on your brush, on the table, or on your clothing. It is, however, the perfect paint to use with papier-mâché because of its permanence and bright colors.

BEADWORK

Beadwork is an art form that has long been associated with the people of Africa. Beads have been a form of trade, commerce, and identification on that continent for thousands of years. Hundreds of years ago, beads were even exchanged for slaves. Some kings were said to have covered their bodies, thrones, stools—everything—with the beads they amassed in the trade of slaves as testimony to their wealth. It is said that one bead was considered so precious that an Ashanti man exchanged it for seven brides.

Beads have been made from shells, glass, seeds, stones, bone, animal teeth, reed, straw, semiprecious stones, bronze, silver, and gold. The following are directions for three necklaces (or bracelets) you can make using everyday materials. Whoever receives your handmade Kwanzaa necklace will probably think it is more valuable than gold.

ITEM: BEADED NECKLACE OR BRACELET

EASY: *1 hour preparation time*

SUPPLIES NEEDED

Elastic bead cording

Large-eyed sewing needle (large enough through which to thread the bead cord but with an eye small enough to pass through the hole of the bead)

Beads, assorted colors

Scissors

Small needle and thread

DIRECTIONS

Determine how long you would like your necklace to be. It should be at least 28" for an adult or at least 24" for a child. Run off a length of cord the size you have chosen plus an

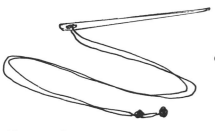

FIGURE 4

additional 5". Thread the needle with the cord, and then knot the ends several times, in two places, about 1" apart so that there are two knots so large the beads cannot slip off. (See Figure 4.) String the beads in a pattern of alternating colors—for example: red, green, yellow, black, white—red, green, yellow, black, white. (See Figure 5.) Or string the colors randomly. Either way, the bright colors of the beads will produce a beautiful effect. After you have beaded the appropriate length, knot the line again and again so the beads cannot fall off. Tie both ends of the necklace together with several knots. Cut off the excess cord and needle 1/2" beyond the knots and sew the ends together with a couple of stitches using a regular sewing needle and thread. (This is to keep the knot, which has been made of slippery elastic thread, from slipping apart.)

For a matching bracelet, simply begin with a 16" cord for an adult or a 12" cord for a child. (Both of these measurements allow for extra cord to make the knots.)

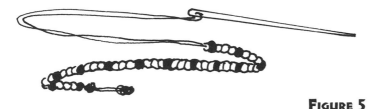

FIGURE 5

ITEM: AFRICAN BEAD NECKLACE

EASY: *1 hour preparation time*

SUPPLIES NEEDED

Bead cording or leather cord strip

Various-sized beads of wood, ceramic, stone, papier-mâché, as well as metal charms such as washers

DIRECTIONS

Thread the beads on the cord using the same lengths as used for the previous necklace (28" plus 5" for an adult and 24" plus 5" for a child). Thread the beads in an interesting pattern. For example, thread one small round wooden bead, one large tubular stone bead, one metal washer, one large wooden bead. Repeat that pattern until you have threaded half of the necklace. Then thread one large charm on the cord (for example, a large, unusual ceramic disk, or a leather or papier-mâché charm). Finish the pattern you started on the first half. Knot and finish the necklace when you get to a good length. The large charm should hang right in the middle of the necklace. When you have finished, you will have made a one-of-a-kind, exotic necklace that anyone in your family will enjoy.

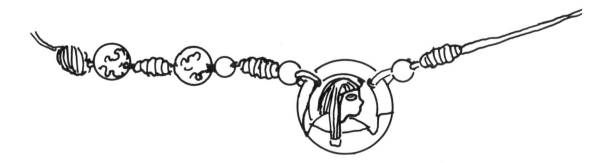

DECORATIVE ITEMS

ITEM: PAPIER-MÂCHÉ MASK (DECORATION OR GIFT)

SKILLED: *4 hours preparation time over 2 days*

SUPPLIES NEEDED

10" paper plates

Pencil

Scissors

Paintbrushes

Small bag of wallpaper paste powder

Bucket

Scrap paper cut into strips and 2" squares

Acrylic gesso, acrylic paints

Picture hanging wire

DIRECTIONS

These masks should be used for wall decorations only because they would be too heavy and restrictive for a person to wear. Draw the face of your mask on the

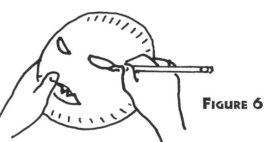

FIGURE 6

paper plate. (See Figure 6.) Cut out the circles or ovals for the eyes and the mouth slightly larger than they will appear in the finished mask. (See Figure 7.)

After you have covered your working surface with newspaper, and you are wearing old clothes, mix about 1/2 cup

FIGURE 7

of the wallpaper paste powder with water so that it is the consistency of a thin paste. Coat your fingers with the paste and cover the strips and squares of the paper with paste on both sides. Apply to the paper plate until you have created a thickness of at least 1/2". (See Figure 8.) For grimacing masks, you may want to add a thicker wad of papier-mâché to create wrinkles in the forehead or thick cheekbones. Or you can attach a nose shape by taping on a paper nose. (See Figure 9.) Attach a piece of picture hang-ing wire at the top with pasted strips. Smooth the papier-mâché with your wet fingers so there are no rough ridges other than those you intended. Wait two days for the masks to dry. Paint them first with acrylic gesso, and then cover them

FIGURE 8

with exotic designs using the acrylic paints. The beginning of these direc-tions shows some designs you can use. Or use your imagination.

FIGURE 9

ITEM: KITCHEN CLAY

(clay made with items found in your kitchen. This dough is not to be eaten.)

SKILLED: *4 hours preparation time over 2 days*

SUPPLIES NEEDED

2 cups flour

1 cup salt

Poster paint

Water jar

Lacquer and lacquer thinner

Paintbrushes

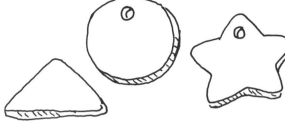

DIRECTIONS

Mix the flour and the salt with a little water until the dough feels a little like modeling clay. Knead the dough on an aluminum foil surface until it is well mixed. Add water if the dough is too dry or flour if it is too sticky.

FIGURE 10

Shape the dough into different figures by starting with balls, rolls, or shapes cut from a rolled-out slab. (See Figure 10.) Or use cookie cutters to create shapes. You can inscribe lines on the sculpture with pencils, or press different textures into the clay. (See Figure 11.) Let the clay dry overnight.

For beads, you can roll out 30 to 40 balls or tubular shapes. Thread the balls onto straws and let the clay dry at least overnight.

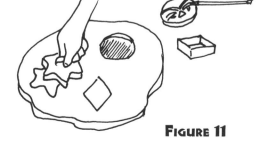

FIGURE 11

Bake the clay in the oven at 200° until it is very hard. Paint on designs using poster paint, and then cover with lacquer. Have an adult help you clean your paintbrushes with lacquer thinner, as it is very messy.

MUSICAL INSTRUMENTS

An important medium of aesthetic expression in Africa is music. Among the principal musical instruments developed in Africa were the xylophone, drum, guitar, zither, harp, and flute. The most frequently used musical form was the song.

We can make simple musical instruments from objects found around the house. They can be given as gifts or used to entertain family and guests at the Karamu, or feast, on the evening of December 31.

Rain sticks are entertaining and beautiful-sounding instruments used by cultures all over the world. They are usually made of local materials available to each culture, such as cactus and seeds or beans in the desert, or long tubular gourds and seeds in Africa. The seeds cascade down metal pins or nails inserted in the sides of the gourds. When the gourds are slowly tilted, the sound the seeds make while falling against the metal is a soft, melodious tinkling that sounds like falling rain.

ITEM: RAIN STICKS

SKILLED: *5 hours preparation time over 2 days*

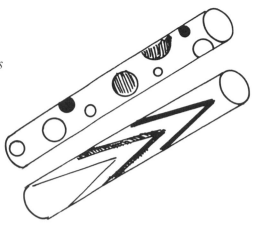

SUPPLIES NEEDED

Cardboard tubes like those from
    wrapping paper (12" or longer)

Sheet of cardboard

Package of straight pins

Masking tape

Wallpaper paste powder

1/2 to 1 cup of uncooked rice kernels

Scrap paper torn into 4" strips

Bucket

Acrylic gesso, acrylic paints

Paintbrushes

Scissors

DIRECTIONS

FIGURE 12

Trace the end of the tube on a sheet of
cardboard twice, then cut out the two
circles, making sure they fit snugly on
the end of the tubes. (See Figure
12.) Cover one end of your tube
with a cardboard circle and
tape it on, making sure
the seal is tight. Insert a
half cup to a full cup of dry
rice in the tube. Cover the

GIFTS TO
MAKE FOR
KWANZAA

other end of the tube with the second cardboard circle and tape it on securely. (See Figure 13.)

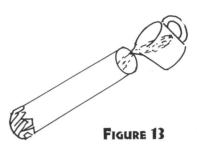

FIGURE 13

Insert the common pins throughout the sides of the tube so they are an equal distance apart and cover the entire tube, say every 1/2". (See Figure 14.)

At this point you should be working on a table that is covered with newspapers, and working in old clothes or an apron because this part of the process can be very messy. Prepare the wallpaper paste by putting a half cup of the dry powder in a plastic bucket. Add enough water and stir with your hand until it is the consistency of a thin paste.

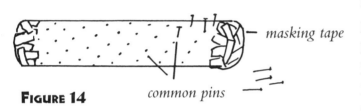

— *masking tape*

FIGURE 14   *common pins* —

Pull strips of torn paper between your glue-filled fingers so that they are covered by the paste and wrap the strips carefully and evenly around the cardboard tube, making sure that the pins are held securely in the tube. You should cover the rain stick completely, including both ends, with the glue-covered paper strips several times in several directions. (See Figure 15.)

The papier-mâché covering should be at least 1/4" thick. Rough spots and bumps should be smoothed down with your wet finger and paste until the surface of the rain stick is relatively smooth. Allow the rain stick two days to dry.

Paint the stick in acrylic gesso, and then acrylic paints, using your own design, or any of the designs at the beginning of this set of instructions.

FIGURE 15

ITEM: PAPIER-MÂCHÉ RATTLES

EASY: *3 hours preparation time over 2 days*

SUPPLIES NEEDED

Small balloons

Rubber bands

Wallpaper paste powder

Bucket

Strips of paper

Seeds or unpopped popcorn

A 5" long by 1/2" wide wooden stick

DIRECTIONS

Blow up a balloon, and tie the end with a rubber band. Add enough water to the wallpaper paste powder in the bucket to create a paste. Slather strips of paper with the wallpaper paste using your fingers. Wrap the strips around the balloon until it is completely covered several times, except for the rubber band end. Form a collar of papier-mâché about 5/8" wide at the rubber band end. (See Figure 16.) Allow two full days to dry.

FIGURE 16

Remove the rubber band, and let the air out of the balloon. Pull the balloon out of the papier-mâché shape. Drop in the seeds or popcorn. Place the end of the stick in the hole and secure with glue. Paint a coating of gesso over the papier-mâché. Paint designs on the rattle with acrylic paint. Wrap yarn or a multicolored cord around the collar at the top of the stick for decoration.

TEXTILES

African textiles take many forms, from Senufo mud cloth, which is a dance and hunting clothing hand decorated with mystical paintings, to imitation kente cloth, which is mass produced today using highly modern technical equipment.

SENUFO MUD CLOTH PAINTINGS

The Senufo tribe of the Ivory Coast uses black mud to paint the images of crocodiles, birds, turtles, fish, and other animals on strips of cotton cloth. Hunters use the fabric as clothing for camouflage because the black-and-white patterns are difficult to see among the trees and undergrowth. The animal figures are believed to be a protection against danger and to help the hunter bring in a large catch.

ITEM: SENUFO MUD PAINTINGS

SKILLED: *4 hours preparation time*

SUPPLIES NEEDED

Pencil

Paper

Black or brown felt-tip marker

A 12" x 24" (or larger if you like) heavyweight cream-colored cotton duck cloth

foamboard

Stapler

Sewing needle and off-white thread

Dark brown or black brush-on fabric dye

Small pans for dye and water

Paintbrushes

DIRECTIONS

Using a pattern from the beginning of this project or below, or one of your own choosing, design your mud painting on paper with a marker. Make your design so the figures of animals and plants fill the page. Staple your duck cloth to the foamboard. Redraw your design on the duck cloth with a pencil. When you are happy with your design, paint over your pencil line with the fabric dye diluted with a little water. Allow the painting time to dry. Remove the staples, and then have an adult help you hem the edges of your painting with a needle and thread. The mud painting can be hung on the wall near your Kwanzaa table.

KENTE CLOTH

Kente cloth is handwoven on narrow looms into strips which are then sewn together. The cloth is made by the Asante people of Ghana and the Ewe people of Ghana and Togo.

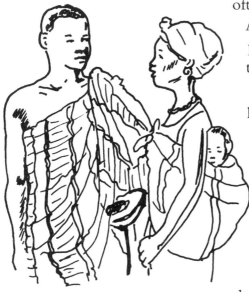

Europeans, arriving in Africa as early as the fifteenth century, began to notice the finely woven cloth, and would often trade their own cloth for it. The Africans would unravel the imported fabrics, particularly fine silk, and rework the textiles to satisfy their own tastes.

Authentic kente cloth is woven into patterns which have been handed down over the centuries. Each pattern has a name that usually refers to a proverb. The patterns vary from simple to highly complex, and the wearing of kente cloth can signify wealth, prestige, occupation, social status, or the significance of the occasion.

When kente patterns are printed on large bolts of cloth and are cut and sewn to make tailored garments, they are not true kente garments. Authentic kente cloth is still woven into strips and sewn together to create a rectangular strip of fabric. On men, the fabric is worn toga-style. On women, the rectangle is worn in a variety of ways; sometimes as a cloth wrapped around the torso or around the body to support a baby on the woman's back.

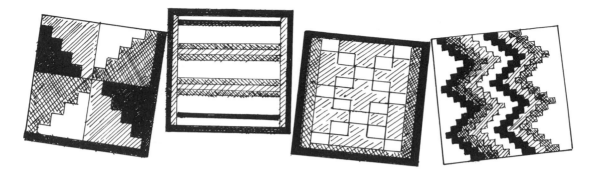

ITEM: KENTE PATTERN NEEDLEPOINT SQUARES

SKILLED: *3 hours preparation time*

SUPPLIES NEEDED

4 3" x 3" 7-mesh plastic canvas squares
   (7 squares to the inch)

4-ply knitting yarn: 1 skein each of green, red, black,
   and yellow

Large-eyed tapestry needles

DIRECTIONS

These are the same patterns that are used in the Kente
Cloth Needlepoint project that follows. This project, however, is much smaller and easier to finish. Also, the pattern is
the same size as your needlepoint and should be easier to
read and compare to your stitching. If you are new to
needlepoint, you can easily tackle the larger project once
you become proficient at following these smaller squares.
Use the designs in Figure 17 as your guide.

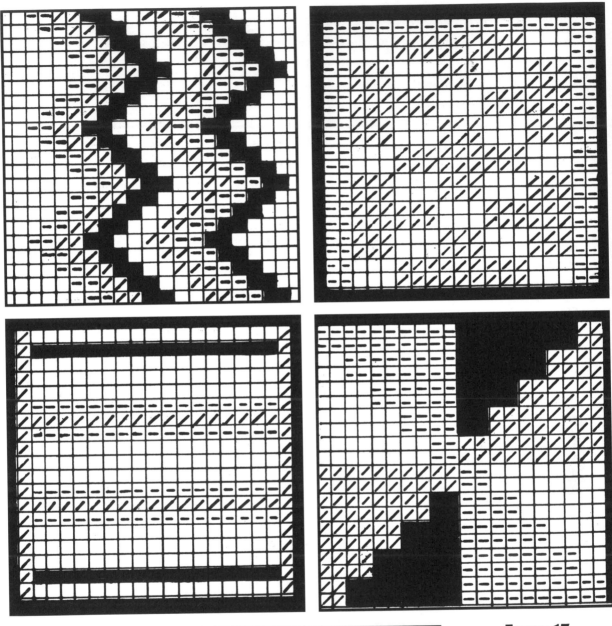

FIGURE 17

COLOR KEY
- ■ BLACK
- □ YELLOW
- — GREEN
- / RED

Transfer the pattern onto your canvas by counting the squares on the pattern and then counting the squares on your canvas. Each square on the pattern equals a hole in the canvas. Use the color key to determine where each color goes, or pick your own colors.

Thread the tapestry needle with a single strand of yarn. Use a half-cross stitch to follow the pattern. (See Figure 18.) This is a simple stitch that is always worked from left to right. Start the stitch at the bottom of the square. Cross over one row of squares diagonally and insert the needle through the hole. The needle is always inserted vertically and all stitches must cross diagonally. When a section of color is completed, do not make a knot. Weave the end of the yarn under a stitch or two in the back. Start a new color by weaving the new ends into a portion in the back you have already completed. Finish the outside of the square with an overcast stitch, which is a series of slanted stitches that covers the edge. You may have to put three overcast stitches in the corners to make sure they are covered. (See Figure 19.) When you have finished all the stitching, cut off all the dangling ends of yarn on the back.

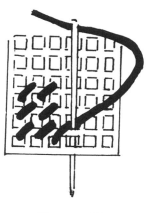

FIGURE 18

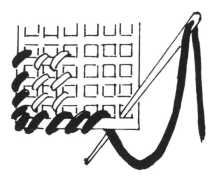

FIGURE 19

The squares may be used as coasters to protect table surfaces, decorations for the Kwanzaa table, or as jewelry with the addition of a safety pin or jewelry pin on the back.

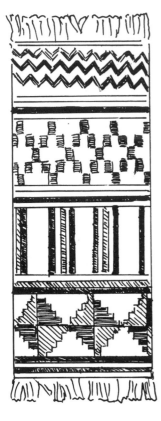

ITEM: KENTE CLOTH NEEDLEPOINT WALL HANGING

CHALLENGE: *30 hours preparation time*

SUPPLIES NEEDED

12" x 24" piece of 7-mesh plastic canvas
   (7 squares to the inch)

4-ply knitting yarn: 1 skein each in aqua blue, red,
   green, black, yellow, gold, and white

Scissors

Large-eyed tapestry needles

Heavyweight cardboard panel 5" square

DIRECTIONS

Use the design and color key shown in Figure 20 as your guide. Transfer the pattern onto your canvas by counting the squares on the pattern, and then counting the squares on your canvas. Each square on the pattern equals a hole in the canvas.

Leave a 1" margin of unstitched canvas. Thread the tapestry needle with a single strand of yarn. Use a half-cross stitch for this pattern as you did for the previous project. (See Figure 18.)

When the section of color is completed, do not make a knot. Weave the end of the yarn under a stitch or two in the back. Start a new color by weaving the new ends into a portion you have already completed. You can make this needlepoint as big as you want by repeating the pattern. After you have finished the stitching, cut off the excess canvas leaving just one row of unstitched canvas. Finish the

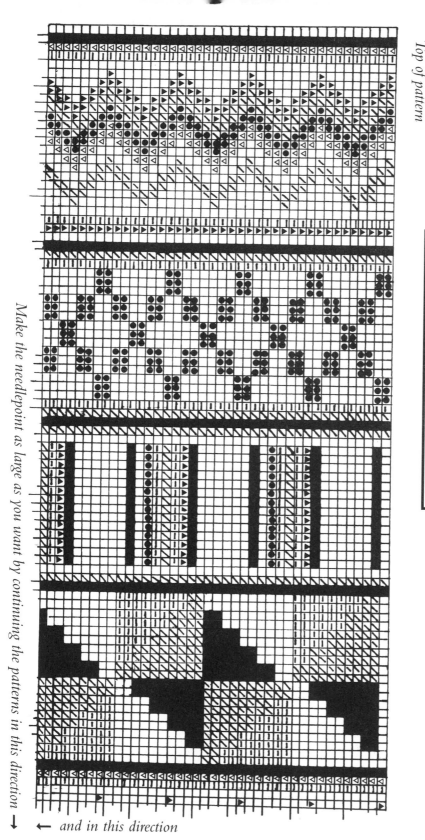

Top of pattern

Make the needlepoint as large as you want by continuing the patterns in this direction →

← *and in this direction*

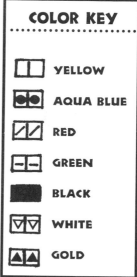

FIGURE 20

COLOR KEY
. . . .

| | YELLOW

AQUA BLUE

RED

GREEN

BLACK

WHITE

GOLD

GIFTS TO MAKE FOR KWANZAA
. . . .

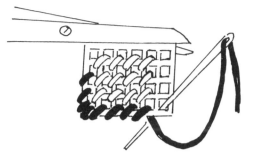

FIGURE 21

unstitched row on the top and bottom of the needlepoint with an overcast stitch, which is a series of slanting stitches that covers the edge. (See Figure 21.) The two sides of the needlepoint will be fringed. Trim off all dangling pieces of yarn on the backside of the stitching.

Wrap the aqua blue yarn around the 5" cardboard square several times, then cut one end. (See Figure 22.) You are creating 10" lengths of yarn, which, when folded in half, will be 5" long fringe. Poke the loop of the fringe from the face of the hanging through the holes in the bottom row through the back. Pull the ends of the fringe through the loop and pull taut. (See Figure 23.) Place fringe only on each end of the needlepoint. (See the drawing at the beginning of this project.)

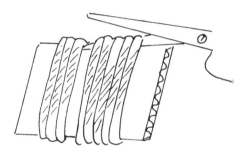

FIGURE 22

FIGURE 23

APPLIQUÉ

Applied felt decoration was in use by tribes in the Gobi Desert as early as 200 B.C. When appliqué was used in Africa, it was usually intended to decorate the surroundings of a king or to commemorate wartime exploits.

Usually appliqué is created when brightly colored shapes are cut out of cotton cloth and basted in place on a black cotton background. Embroidery is often used to fill in the details. In the following instructions, we will cut shapes out of various colored felt pieces and glue them to a black background. If you are an accomplished sewer, or can get help from someone who is, try sewing the figures onto the background like Africans have been doing for thousands of years.

ITEM: APPLIQUÉ MURAL

SKILLED: *6 hours preparation time*

SUPPLIES NEEDED

Felt: 1 red piece and 1 black piece, each 18" x 24"; 1 yellow piece, 9" x 24"

8 to 10 9" x 12" pieces of felt in various colors

Scissors

Common pins

Sewing needle

Transparent polyester thread

Bottle of white glue or glue gun and glue sticks

Ruler

3/4" wooden dowel

Sewing machine (optional)

DIRECTIONS

Cut a strip of red felt that is 24" long by 4" wide. Pin one edge to the top 1" of the black felt along the 24" length. (See Figure 24.) Fold the red felt in half and then sew it to the black felt by hand or have an adult sew it by machine,

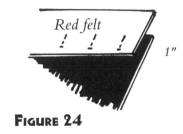

Red felt

1"

FIGURE 24

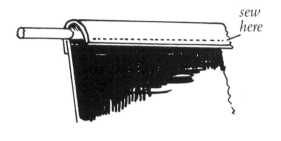

sew here

FIGURE 25

creating a sleeve that is at least 1 1/2" wide, large enough to hold a 3/4" wooden dowel. (See Figure 25.) Cut another red strip that is 24" long by 4" wide, fold it in half and pin and sew it to the other end of the black felt. You can also make a strip of yellow triangles from the pattern that follows on page 100 and sew them in place across the red sleeve seams. (See Figure 26.)

Select animals and other shapes from the patterns on the following pages. Enlarge these patterns on a photocopy machine up to 200%, making three enlarged copies of each

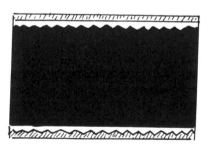

FIGURE 26

pattern. Using one of the copies, cut out the large pattern shape and pin it to the color of felt you plan to use. (For example, if you are going to make a blue elephant with pink ears and a green-and-yellow blanket, you would first cut out the entire elephant pattern by cutting along the thick black line and pin it to the blue felt.) Now cut the shape out of the felt. Cut the medium-sized pattern pieces apart from the second photocopy. Cut the smallest shapes (for example, the top blanket shape) from the third photocopy. Attach these pattern pieces with pins to the appropriate colors of felt for the

common pins

FIGURE 27

details. (See Figure 27.) Cut out these shapes and glue them to the large felt shape. (See Figure 28.) If you plan to make more than one of the same animal, glue the pattern to poster board to make it stronger, and then cut out the patterns.

Assemble the other shapes on the black felt in a pleasing way. African wall hangings are usually full of colorful figures and shapes that fill virtually the whole picture plane. Once you are satisfied with your design, you can glue the pieces in place.

Slip the dowel inside the sleeve you have created in the red panel. Tie string around each end of the dowel, so you can hang the appliqué near your Kwanzaa table. You will have used Kuumba to create a one-of-a-kind decoration to enhance the Kwanzaa celebration.

FIGURE 28

This is the pattern for the yellow triangles. Pin to folded felt to make a double length.

PAPER CRAFTS

While items produced on paper are not necessarily considered an African craft (even the storytelling tradition has, until recently, been exclusively oral), there are many wonderful gift items that can be created with paper. The first project will describe how to create unique personally designed paper to wrap all the wonderful gifts you have already created. Other projects will include making prints, greeting cards, and books.

ITEM: WRAPPING PAPER

EASY: *1 hour preparation time*

SUPPLIES NEEDED

Styrofoam meat trays, preferably with flat surfaces

Cardboard

Scissors

Stapler

Long sheets or rolls of bond or brown wrapping paper

DIRECTIONS

Draw different designs of various shapes and sizes on the Styrofoam trays, trying to avoid any textures already inscribed on the trays. The easiest designs to work with are

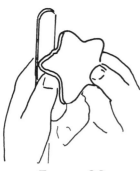

FIGURE 29

no smaller than 1 1/2" and no larger than 4" in diameter. Cut your drawings out with scissors. You can refine your designs using sandpaper or an emery board. (See Figure 29.) Cut strips of cardboard that are 4 1/2" long and 1/2" wide. Fold each cardboard strip 2" from the right end, and again, 2" from the left. (There should be a 1/2" space between the two folds. See Figure 30.) Staple the center of the cardboard strips two or three times to the Styrofoam shapes, leaving the long ends free as handles. The staples should not interfere with the printed design. (See Figure 31.)

Fill unused trays with a layer of acrylic or poster paints. Dip the Styrofoam shapes into the paint, and then press various patterns onto the rolls of paper. (See Figure 32.) Allow time for the paint to dry before you try to wrap presents. You can also use this method to decorate greeting cards.

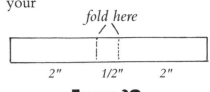

fold here

2"   1/2"   2"

FIGURE 30

FIGURE 31

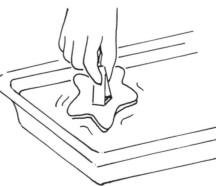

FIGURE 32

GIFTS TO
MAKE FOR
KWANZAA

ITEM: MARBLED PAPERS

SKILLED: *2 hours preparation time*

SUPPLIES NEEDED

A pan that is at least 3" deep, like an old roasting pan or a dishwashing pan

Bottle of liquid starch

Large-toothed comb or pick

Clean bond paper cut smaller than the pan by 1"

Tubes of oil paint

Jars for mixing paint

Turpentine

A plastic spoon for each color

Scrap newspaper

Pencil

A pan or bucket of clean water

DIRECTIONS

Cover the top of your worktable with newspaper. Fill the pan with liquid starch 2" to 3" deep. Determine what you would like to use the marbled paper for, whether as endpapers for a book, wrapping paper, or a sheet of bookmarks, and cut sheets of bond paper slightly larger than that size. (For example, a book that is 4" x 5" would need two cover sheets that are at least 5" x 6", and two endpaper sheets that are 4" x 5" each.) Put a dab of each color of oil paint in individual jars. Dilute these dabs with turpentine and stir with clean plastic spoons until the paint is the consistency of melted ice cream—fluid, but not runny. Take spoonfuls of this diluted paint and drop them randomly onto the top layer of the starch.

The drops could be as small as 1/8" in diameter, but should be no larger than 1" wide. If the color starts to spread and get thin, you are using too much turpentine. If the paint is too thin, add more paint from the tube to your paint jar. If the paint is too thick, it will drop to the bottom of the pan. Add more turpentine to the paint jar.

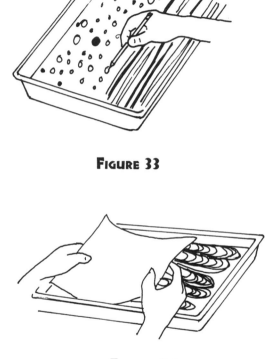

FIGURE 33

Spoon drops of at least one other color on the starch. Ten or fifteen drops of each color can make a beautiful pattern. Draw through the drops in a straight line or in a zigzag design with a pencil. (See Figure 33.) Then you can take the pick or comb and rake through those colors in a different direction to create another pattern. Try not to draw through these drops more than two or three times or the colors will mix together and simply get muddy. Each color should retain its character in its pattern on top of the starch.

FIGURE 34

Lay your clean paper slowly on top of the paint pattern (See Figure 34), being careful not to trap any air pockets between the paper and paint. If the paper is thin enough, you can probably see the pattern from the reverse side. Lift it off carefully, letting the surplus paint and starch drip

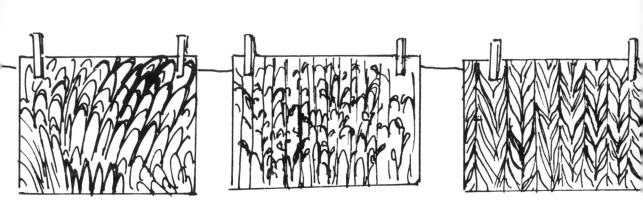

ASSORTED MARBLE PATTERNS

off into the starch pan, and then submerge the newly patterned print in a pan of clean water or rinse under a water faucet. The extra starch, and not the painting, will wash away.

Hang the printed sheet on a clothesline, or lay it on clean newspaper placed on the floor for this purpose. The print will be dry enough to handle in about an hour, but the oil paint will not be completely dry for at least 24 hours. Make sure the print does not dry sticking to the newspaper. You can place the dry prints under heavy books or between the pages of phone books to flatten them, as long as the print side is protected with a layer of clean paper.

To make additional prints, clean any stray oil droplets off the top layer of starch with folded newspaper, and then add more drops of paint for the next pattern. You can experiment with the number of colors you use or your zigzag comb work. As more and more prints are made, you may have to add more starch to the pan. If you use a water pan to clean the prints, you will have to change the water after every sixth print or so.

ITEM: POP-UP GREETING CARDS

SKILLED: *1 hour preparation time*

SUPPLIES NEEDED

Construction or art paper, assorted colors, 9" x 12"

Pencil

Ruler

Paper glue

Scissors

Assorted colored markers

DIRECTIONS

Pick out two colors of construction paper. Fold both in half so that the two sheets of paper are now 6" x 9". Put aside the color you are using for the outside of the card. On the fold of the inside color sheet, measure and mark with a pencil a rectangle that is 1 1/2" x 4" (See Figure 35.) With a pair of scissors, cut the two sides of the box, but not the top 4" line. (See Figure 36.) This is the portion of the card that pops up.

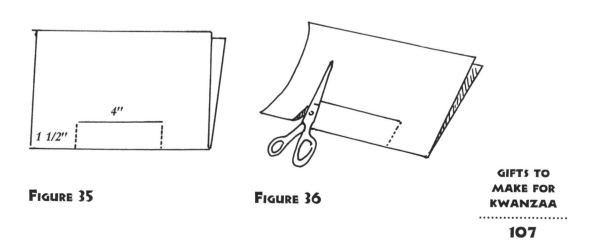

FIGURE 35

4"

1 1/2"

FIGURE 36

FIGURE 37

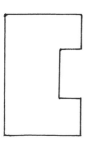

FIGURE 38

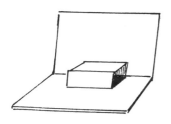

FIGURE 39

Hold the card in one hand and use your index finger of the other hand to push out the rectangle that you created so that it folds in the opposite direction. (See Figure 37.) Fold the card flat along the 4" pencil line still indicated on the sheet. The card should look like Figure 38 when folded and like Figure 39 when opened.

Glue your second sheet of paper to the back side of the pop-up sheet. Be careful not to glue down the pop-up tent you have created. Use shapes cut from other colored papers to create animals, trees, people, masks, or other objects you want to pop up. See the cards at the beginning of these instructions for examples. Make sure whatever shapes you glue to the tent do not interfere with the opening and closing of your card.

Write a poem, joke, or invitation with the markers or colored pencils on the outside of the card. On the inside, write the response. For example, look at the card pictured below. (Outside) "What did the cat say to his friends when he wanted them to come over for Kwanzaa Karamu?" (Inside) "I'm not lion. Come on over at 7 P.M. on December 31 for our Kwanzaa feast!" If you like, you can buy envelopes in which to mail your cards in most stationery stores.

BOOKS

There are many kinds of handmade books you can make to give as gifts. You can make your own comic books, write your own picture book, or even record the words to your own songs or poetry. Perhaps your father is inspired by the words of Malcolm X. Imagine how delighted he would be if you went to the library and found quotes from Malcolm X's speeches and inscribed them in a book you made by hand. Or you can make any book that suits your fancy. Use the following instructions to learn how to make a handmade book. If you run out of time, or would simply prefer an easier craft, you can go to a store and buy a ready-made book or notebook to fill with your writing. The words you put on the pages are the most important element in creating a Kwanzaa gift book.

ITEM: ACCORDION BOOK

SKILLED: *2 hours preparation time*

SUPPLIES NEEDED

A large sheet of white drawing paper, preferably 19" x 24", cut into 4 strips that are 4" x 24". (There will be a waste paper strip that is 3" x 24".)

Scissors

Ruler

Pencil, assorted markers, colored pencils, etc.

2 pieces of cardboard each cut to 4 1/4" x 4 1/4"

2 decorated or colored sheets such as marbled paper
at least 5" x 5" for the covers. (Or you may want to
do a separate drawing for the front cover.)

2 decorated or colored sheets such as marbled paper at
least 4 1/8" x 4 1/8" for endpapers

DIRECTIONS

Lightly mark with pencil every 4" on both long edges of the
4" x 24" paper strips. This indicates six panels. Make a sharp
straight crease on these marks by folding the paper against
the ruler. (See Figure 40.)

Open up the strip and refold the panels like an accordion.
(See Figure 41.) If you use only this one strip of
paper, you will create a book that has four panels. (The other two panels will be glued to the
inside covers of the books.) This would be a
good time to decorate, design, and fill out the
writing you would like on the pages of your

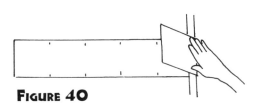

FIGURE 40

book. If you would like to make a
nine-panel book, you can glue the
two folded strips together by adding
another strip as in Figure 42. Do
not decorate the first and last panels.

Center your two 4 1/4" cardboard squares on the back side of

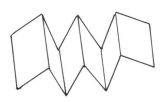

FIGURE 41

your two 5" cover squares of paper. Fold the edges of the
cover paper over the cardboard squares. Remove the cardboard, and then cut the corners with a scissors as in Figure 43. This removes the
excess paper. Glue and fold over just one of
the flaps on the cardboard. (See Figure 44.)

Glue one of the ends of the accordion
strip onto the undecorated side of one of

FIGURE 42

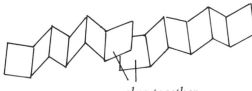

glue together

the covers, making sure it is perfectly centered (See Figure 45), then glue down the other three cover flaps. Glue one of the endpaper squares, which should be slightly smaller than the cover, precisely on top of this panel. This is the only gluing which will hold the pages into the book. (See Figure 46.) Repeat these steps for the other end panel of the book. After you have finished gluing the book together, make sure all of the excess glue has been wiped clean, and then place the closed, folded book under a large weight, like a phone book, to dry for a few hours.

Use your newly made books to write down your Kwanzaa memories and to enclose your photos, keepsakes, writings, and drawings. Use the new book to record your family's history. Or use your book as a gift to give to a family member so he or she can record daily experiences and thoughts. All of these crafts are part of Kuumba, and therefore a wonderful part of Kwanzaa.

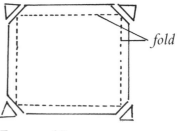

FIGURE 43

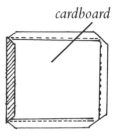

cardboard

FIGURE 44

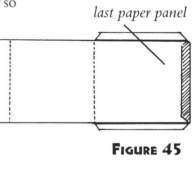

last paper panel

FIGURE 45

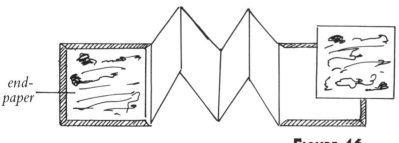

end-paper

FIGURE 46

TOYS

The following instructions will teach you how to make hand puppets and dolls you can use to entertain during Kwanzaa observances, to give as gifts to other children, or simply to keep for your own enjoyment.

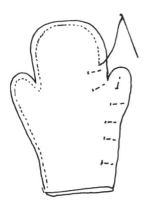

ITEM: HAND PUPPETS

EASY: *1 hour preparation time for each puppet*

SUPPLIES NEEDED

Paper

Pencil

Common pins

Assorted colors of felt

Sewing needle and thread

A bottle of white glue or a glue gun

DIRECTIONS

Place your hand over the pattern on page 113 (Figure 47). If there is plenty of room for your hand to move freely, then make a photocopy of the pattern at its present size, or enlarge it slightly if it is too small. If you are making a puppet for an adult, make a photocopy of the pattern at 120% and cut it out. Attach the pattern to two pieces of felt with common pins, and cut out the puppet hand shapes. Sew them together with a needle and thread allowing for a 1/2" seam. (See Figure 48.)

Use the animals designs on pages 114 and 115 to decorate your puppets or create some designs of your own. If you use these designs, photocopy them at 225% for a child's puppet (for most copy machines, you'll first need to copy the design at 150%, then copy the resulting image again at 150%), or 270% for an adult's puppet (copy the design as you would for a child, then copy the resulting image again at 120%). Cut out the pattern pieces and pin them to the appropriate color of felt. Assemble the felt pieces on top of the puppet shapes. When you are happy with the arrangement, glue the felt pieces down. The pieces will stay on

FIGURE 48

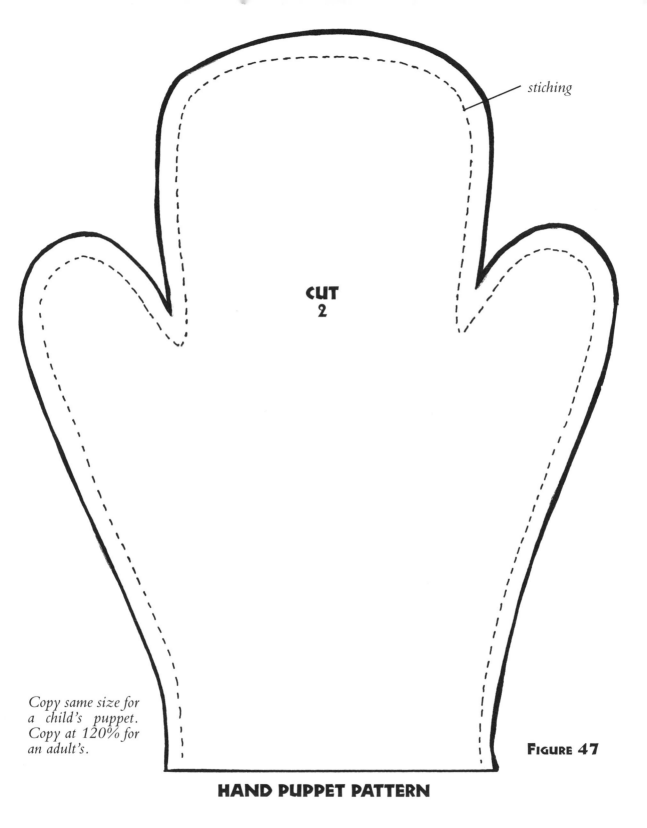

stiching

**CUT
2**

*Copy same size for
a child's puppet.
Copy at 120% for
an adult's.*

FIGURE 47

HAND PUPPET PATTERN

HAND PUPPET DESIGNS

Copy at 225% for a child's puppet, or

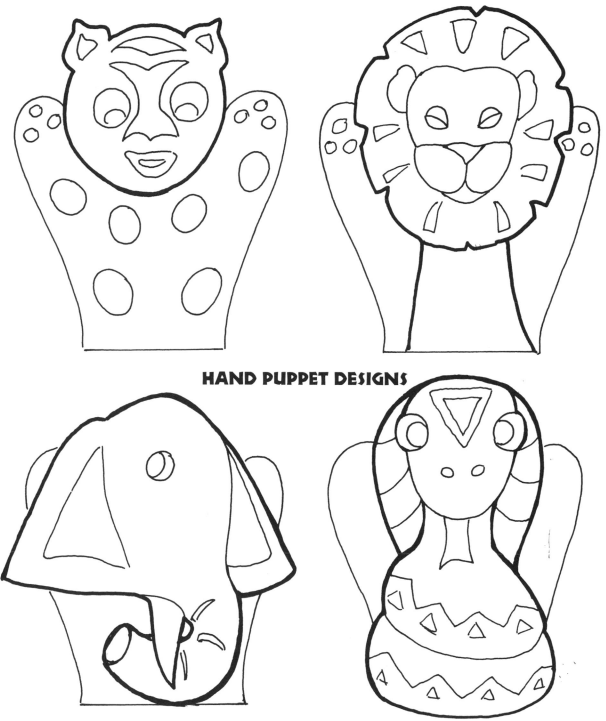

HAND PUPPET DESIGNS

copy at 270% for an adult's puppet.

more securely if you have an adult help you glue them on with a glue gun. You can make a whole menagerie of animal characters and perform your own play.

ITEM: HANDMADE DOLL

SKILLED: *3 hours preparation time*

SUPPLIES NEEDED

Scissors

12" black or brown muslin or cotton brocade

Common pins

Pencil

Sewing needle and assorted colored threads

Sewing machine (optional)

Scraps of material with African-inspired designs

Fiberfill stuffing or old nylon stockings

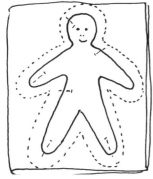

FIGURE 50

FIGURE 51

DIRECTIONS

Make a photocopy of the pattern that follows (Figure 49). Cut out the pattern along the dotted lines. Fold the muslin in two and attach the pattern to it with common pins. Cut out the two doll pieces. (See Figure 50.)

Decorate the face of the doll by indicating with a pencil where the eyes, nose, and mouth should be on one of the doll pieces. On the back side of the face, stitch in a few stitches in black for the eyes, a row of red stitches for the mouth, and perhaps a couple of black stitches for the nostrils. (See Figure 51.) Pin front sides of the pieces together and then sew them with a needle and thread (or ask an adult

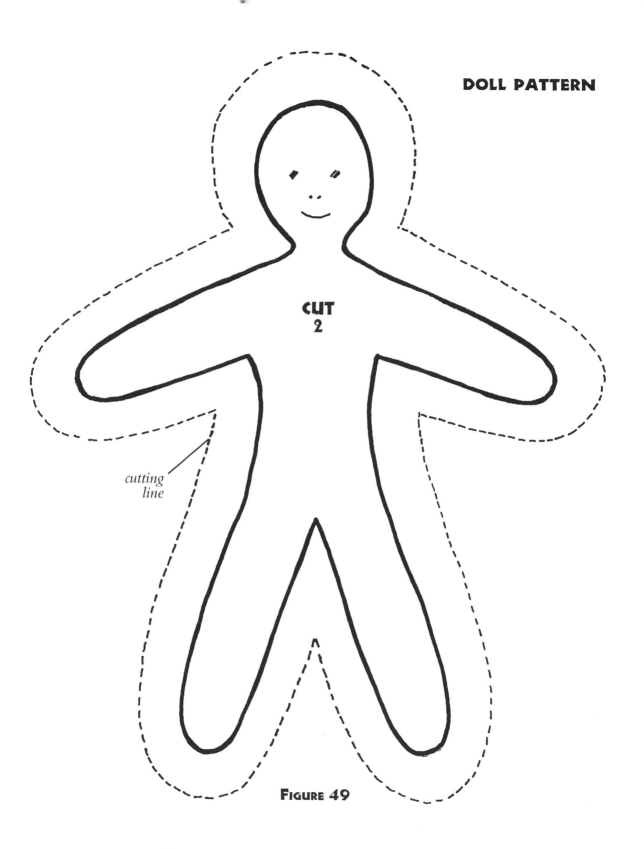

DOLL PATTERN

CUT
2

cutting
line

FIGURE 49

to sew them together on a sewing machine), allowing for a 1/2" seam. Leave one of the side seams open from armpit to hip. Have the adult trim the seam to 1/4", and then snip the seam allowance (which is the 1/4" of material left from stitching to edge) at 1" intervals, particularly around curves.

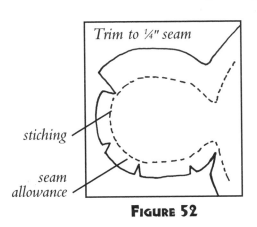

Trim to ¼" seam

stiching

seam allowance

FIGURE 52

(See Figure 52.) Turn the doll inside out and stuff her with fiberfill or pieces of old nylon stockings. (See Figure 53.) A pencil might help you get the stuffing in the narrow arm, leg, and head shapes. Sew the open seam closed by hand using an overcast stitch. (See Figure 54.)

Drape Africa-inspired cloth swatches around the torso as a dress and around the doll's head as a wrap. Make small hidden stitches to hold the cloth wraps on, or just tie on the clothing so that it can be changed at will.

The recipient of this, or of any of the other crafts in this chapter, will undoubtedly appreciate how much time, devotion, love, and Kuumba you expended to create this project. It will probably always be a treasured Kwanzaa keepsake.

FIGURE 53

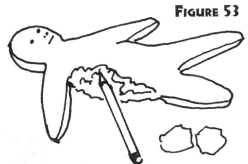

FIGURE 54

CHAPTER SIX

RECIPES FOR A
WELL-FED KWANZAA

A meal well made is a gift to savor.
—Ancient proverb

WHAT FOODS CAN
I PREPARE FOR KWANZAA?

The food prepared for the week of Kwanzaa, as well as the Karamu on the night of December 31, should be like all meals—healthy, nutritious, and delicious. But you can apply special consideration to meals cooked for Kwanzaa. You can experiment and prepare dishes that you or your parents might not ordinarily cook, such as dishes from Africa and traditional African American dishes.

Some of the recipes are complex and will involve continuous adult supervision. Some of the recipes are simple and easy enough for children to make from start to finish virtually by themselves. But with each recipe, make sure there is an adult close by for guidance, to use any electric mixers or food processors, or even to help with the cooking. They might even offer some of their own recipes to add to the feast.

A suggested menu is included at the end of the chapter so that you can create an entire Kwanzaa feast for your family and guests.

APPETIZERS/SALADS

Fruits and vegetables, where available, have long played a large part in the African diet. Their color, flavor, and nutritional value often enhance any snack or meal.

DISH: FRUIT-IN-SEASON SALAD

EASY: *1/2 hour preparation time*

INGREDIENTS

2 large oranges, peeled, sectioned, and seeded

2 large bananas, sliced

2 large pears, cored and sectioned

3 apples, cored and sectioned

1 cup seedless grapes

1 cup orange juice

DIRECTIONS

Place the fruit in a large bowl, and toss gently with orange juice to prevent fruit from browning. Cover fruit, and chill in refrigerator until just before serving.

DISH: GREEN SALAD

EASY: *1/2 hour preparation time*

INGREDIENTS

6 cups various lettuce leaves (iceberg, butter, etc.)

1 medium tomato and 1 large cucumber, sliced

Bottled salad dressing

DIRECTIONS

Tear lettuce leaves into bite-sized pieces, and then rinse in a colander under water. Allow lettuce to drain dry. Place lettuce in large bowl and cover with a damp paper towel. Cover bowl and place in refrigerator to chill. Just before serving, add sliced tomato and cucumber. Provide bottled dressings for your guests.

MAIN DISHES

A traditional African American dish for New Year's Day is Hoppin' John—or black-eyed peas and rice. Thought to bring luck, this dish is prepared in many homes for the start of the New Year. The following is a recipe for lovers of a spicier black-eyed peas with sausage. If you plan to prepare this recipe using dried black-eyed peas, you must allow an extra day to prepare the dish because you will need to soak the peas overnight.

DISH: SPICY HOPPIN' JOHN (BLACK-EYED PEAS AND RICE)

CHALLENGE: *1/2 hour preparation time,*
1 1/2 hours cooking time

INGREDIENTS

1 pound dried black-eyed peas, 5 cups water

1 cup uncooked rice

l pound low-fat sausage such as smoked sausage or kielbasa

1 medium-size onion, chopped

1/2 cup chopped celery

1 medium garlic clove, minced

1 medium green bell pepper, seeded, chopped

2 10-ounce cans chunky tomatoes & green chiles

1 teaspoon salt (optional)

1 teaspoon ground black pepper

DIRECTIONS

Place peas in large bowl and soak them in water overnight. Pour peas into a colander and rinse them thoroughly with cold running water, picking through and discarding shriveled, broken, or discolored peas.

In large saucepan, cover peas with 5 cups fresh water. Heat the peas until the liquid bubbles to a boil. Reduce heat to low and allow them to simmer until they are tender yet firm—about 40 minutes.

Meanwhile cook 1 cup of rice following package instructions. Slice the sausage into 1/2" pieces. Place the sausage in a large skillet coated with a nonstick finish and brown over low heat. Add the chopped onion, celery, garlic, and bell pepper and sautee until they are only slightly cooked—about 5 minutes.

In the pot with the peas add the sauteed onion/garlic/pepper/sausage mixture, as well as the salt, black pepper, and cans of chunky tomatoes & chiles. Cover tightly and cook over low heat until peas are tender, about 20 more minutes. Serve the peas and sausage over the rice. Makes 6–8 servings.

DISH: TUNA SESAME SALAD

EASY: *40 minutes preparation time*

INGREDIENTS

6 cups various lettuce leaves (iceberg, butter, etc.)

2 6 1/8-ounce cans of solid white tuna in spring water

6 ounces cheddar cheese, cubed

1 cup cherry tomatoes

2 tablespoons sesame seeds

Bottled Italian dressing

DIRECTIONS

Tear lettuce into bite-sized pieces. Rinse lettuce thoroughly in a colander and let dry. Put lettuce into a large salad bowl. Cover with damp paper towel, and then cover the bowl and refrigerate.

Drain the liquid from the tuna cans, and separate the chunks into smaller sections. Just before serving, add the tuna, cheese, washed tomatoes, and sesame seeds to the lettuce bowl and toss. Drizzle the dressing on top of the salad. Serves 4 to 6 as a main dish salad.

DISH: BEEF ROAST

CHALLENGE: *2 hours preparation time*

INGREDIENTS

1 3-pound pot roast

1 teaspoon salt

1/2 teaspoon pepper

1 cup small or cubed white potatoes

1/2 cup each whole baby onions, sliced carrots

DIRECTIONS

Have an adult place the roast in the roasting pan and brown meat on all sides under your oven's broiler a few inches from the heat. Add 1/2 cup water, salt, and pepper. Cover tightly and bake at 325° for 1 1/2 hours, or until tender. Add potatoes, onions, and carrots, and cook an additional 45 minutes. Place roast on a platter and surround it with vegetables. Wait 10 minutes before carving. You can thicken pan juices with flour for gravy.

THE PEANUT

The Portuguese brought the peanut to West Africa in the early 1500s, and by the middle of the century it was already an established crop in Senegal and Gambia. Within 200 years peanuts were being eaten in countries all the way across Africa as far west as Angola, probably because they were so similar to the African "groundnut." They also probably spread so widely because they easily integrated into native dishes.

Peanuts even accompanied African slaves to the Americas. The old American name *goober* comes from the Congolese word *nguba*. In Africa today, peanuts are added to stews with meat, onions, tomatoes, and chiles. In West Africa, it's characteristic to add dried shrimp or fish to groundnut stews.

The following recipe for an American groundnut stew is a delicious mixture of peanut and chicken flavors and textures. If you grind peanuts yourself in a blender or food processor, the flavors will be even further enhanced. It is recommended that you ask an adult to help with the blender and to cut up the chicken.

DISH: GROUNDNUT STEW

CHALLENGE: *40 minutes preparation time,*
1 1/2 hours cooking time

INGREDIENTS

1 (2 1/2–3 pound) stewing chicken, cut up

l inch fresh ginger

1 cup onion chopped

2 cups water

1 medium tomato, coarsely chopped

1 cup peanuts or 2/3 cup crunchy peanut butter

2 tablespoons tomato paste

2 teaspoons salt

1 teaspoon ground black pepper

2 tablespoons cayenne pepper

DIRECTIONS

Rinse the chicken and then pat it dry. Have an adult remove the fat and skin and cut the chicken into 3/4" cubes. Combine the chicken, ginger, chopped onion, chopped tomato, and water in a large saucepan. Cover and bring to a boil. Reduce heat. Simmer for 1 hour.

Meanwhile, if you are using fresh peanuts, have an adult put them in a grinder or food processor to grind them until they are a coarse powder. Put this powder, or your already prepared peanut butter, in a bowl, add broth from chicken stock, and blend. Add back into the chicken pot with tomato paste, salt, and the two kinds of ground peppers. Partially cover and cook on low heat until the chicken is tender, about 30 additional minutes. Add water if sauce gets too thick to maintain a stewlike consistency. Yield: 4–6 servings.

VEGETABLES

DISH: GRACIE'S GREEN BEANS WITH ALMONDS

EASY: *1/2 hour preparation and cooking time*

INGREDIENTS

2 tablespoons butter or margarine

1/2 cup of blanched sliced almonds

1 pound fresh green beans

1/2 package dry onion soup mix

1 tablespoon lemon juice

DIRECTIONS

Brown almonds in the butter in a frying pan over medium heat about 5 minutes. Meanwhile, wash the beans and trim off their ends. Add salt to 2 quarts of water in a saucepan and bring to a boil. Drop in the beans, a few at a time, so the water never stops boiling. This keeps the beans green. If the water should stop boiling, cover the pot until the water boils again. Add the rest of the beans and leave the pot uncovered. Stir the onion soup mix and lemon juice in with the beans, and cook for 6 to 8 minutes, or until beans are tender enough for your taste. Drain the excess water, and serve the beans in a bowl tossed with the almonds and butter.

DISH: CANDIED SWEET POTATOES

SKILLED: *1 hour preparation and cooking time*

INGREDIENTS

6 medium sweet potatoes

1/4 cup butter or margarine

1/4 cup brown sugar

DIRECTIONS

Peel and cut up sweet potatoes into 1-inch cubes. Add the potatoes to boiling water in a saucepan. The water should cover the potatoes by at least 1 inch. Reduce heat, add butter and brown sugar, stir, and then cover. Allow potatoes to cook at medium heat for at least 35 minutes until the juices have thickened into a glaze, and the potatoes are tender. Serves 6.

BREADS

DISH: ZUCCHINI MUFFINS

EASY: *1 hour preparation and baking time*

INGREDIENTS

1 1/2 sticks margarine

3/4 cup sugar

3 tablespoons brown sugar

2 eggs

2 cups all-purpose flour

1 teaspoon ground allspice

3/4 cup buttermilk

1/2 teaspoon salt

1 1/2 teaspoons baking powder

1/4 teaspoon baking soda

1/2 teaspoon vanilla flavoring

1 medium zucchini, grated

DIRECTIONS

In a large bowl, cream margarine and sugar together by stirring with a large spoon. Add eggs, flour, allspice, buttermilk, salt, baking powder, baking soda, and vanilla, and mix. Add grated zucchini to mixture. Pour into baking cups in a muffin tin. Bake for 15 to 20 minutes at 300°.

DISH: CORN BREAD

EASY: *35 minutes preparation and baking time*

INGREDIENTS

1 cup sifted flour

4 teaspoons baking powder

1/2 teaspoon salt

1 cup yellow cornmeal

2 eggs

1 1/4 cups milk

1/4 cup vegetable oil

DIRECTIONS

Sift flour with baking powder and salt. Add to 1 cup of cornmeal in a large bowl. Add eggs, milk, and oil. Stir until all ingredients are moistened, but do not overmix. Pour into a greased 9" square baking pan. Bake in the oven for 15 to 20 minutes at 350°. Cut into 12 squares.

DESSERTS

A good dessert can be the ultimate complement to your Kwanzaa Karamu feast. It can also be the part of the meal children already have some experience making. Enjoy yourself in creating these tasteful treats, because your guests will be enjoying themselves as they experience eating them.

DISH: UNCLE HERBERT'S SPICED BAKED APPLES

EASY: *1 1/2 hours preparation and baking time*

INGREDIENTS

4 Rome baking apples

1/2 cup brown sugar

1/2 cup granulated sugar

1 teaspoon apple cider vinegar

1/2 teaspoon cinnamon

1 cup water

DIRECTIONS

Preheat oven to 475°. Have an adult core the apples. Place in a greased baking pan. Mix the sugars, cinnamon, water, and vinegar together in a small mixing bowl. Fill the holes with the mixture. Bake for 1 hour. Makes 4 servings.

DISH: AMBROSIA

EASY: *40 minutes preparation time*

INGREDIENTS

4 large oranges, peeled, sectioned, and seeded
  or 1 8-ounce can of mandarin oranges

1/2 cup seedless grapes

1 large grapefruit, peeled, sectioned, and seeded

1 16-ounce can of pineapple chunks, drained

2 cups whipped cream or whipped dairy dessert

1 4-ounce bottle maraschino cherries, drained

DIRECTIONS

Combine all fruit in a large bowl. Mix with whipped cream just before serving. Serve on a platter covered with lettuce leaves. Yields 10 servings.

DISH: SUGAR COOKIES

SKILLED: *1 hour preparation and baking time*

INGREDIENTS

3/4 cup granulated sugar

3/4 cup margarine or unsalted butter

1 teaspoon vanilla

1 egg

1 tablespoon milk

2 cups sifted all-purpose flour

1 1/2 teaspoons baking powder

1/4 teaspoon salt

Food coloring or cookie sprinkles

DIRECTIONS

Cream sugar, butter or margarine, and vanilla together in a large bowl. Break egg in a separate cup, and then beat in with the creamed ingredients until light and fluffy. Stir in milk.

Sift together dry ingredients. Blend into creamed mixture to form a stiff dough. Put dough in refrigerator to chill at least 1 hour.

Take about 1/3 of the dough and place it on a sheet of waxed paper or other clean, smooth surface that has been dusted lightly with flour. Return the remainder of the dough to the refrigerator to stay chilled. Roll dough flat with a rolling pin until it is about 1/8" thick. Using cookie cutters, cut out shapes. After you have placed the cookie shapes on the greased cookie pan, you can decorate them by sprinkling them with granulated sugar colored with food coloring.

Another quicker method to form sugar cookies is to roll tablespoon-sized portions of chilled dough into balls between your hands. Place the balls on a greased cookie sheet, and flatten them to 1/8" thick with the bottom of a clean drinking glass. Sprinkle the colored sugar over the cookies before baking. If you'd like, decorate the cookies in Kwanzaa colors—red, green, and black—with precolored candy sprinkles (using chocolate for black). Bake on a greased cookie sheet at 350° for 8 to 10 minutes or until lightly brown. Cool slightly and remove from the pan with a spatula. Makes 3 dozen cookies.

DISH: CHOCOLATE ALMOND COOKIES

EASY: *1 hour preparation time*

INGREDIENTS

1 cup sugar

2 eggs

1/3 cup unsweetened cocoa powder

1 1/2 cups flour

1 teaspoon baking soda

1/2 cup slivered blanched almonds

1/2 teaspoon vegetable oil

DIRECTIONS

Preheat oven to 350°. In a mixing bowl, beat sugar and eggs with a spoon until well mixed. In another bowl, combine the cocoa, flour, baking soda, and almonds. Add this to the sugar and egg mixture. Drop spoonfuls of batter onto a baking sheet greased with vegetable oil. Bake for 15 to 20 minutes.

Let cookies cool in pan for 2 minutes and then remove to wire rack to cool completely. Makes 3 dozen cookies.

DRINKS

You can offer the guests at your Kwanzaa Karamu bottled waters, carbonated beverages, coffee, and tea. But I think they will be most delighted with your menu of holiday drinks.

DRINK: HOT APPLE CIDER

EASY: *1/2 hour preparation time*

INGREDIENTS

2 quarts apple cider

4 cinnamon sticks

DIRECTIONS

Pour 2 quarts of cider into a large pot containing the cinnamon sticks. Stir occasionally as the beverage simmers over medium heat the length of the party. Ladle out portions into eggnog cups.

DRINK: PINEAPPLE SUNRISE PUNCH

EASY: *1/2 hour preparation time*

INGREDIENTS

1 46-ounce can pineapple juice, chilled

1 6-ounce can crushed pineapple

1 2-liter bottle grapefruit-flavored soda

1 cup grenadine syrup

DIRECTIONS

Pour the pineapple juice into a large glass punch bowl filled with ice. Add the crushed pineapple, some of the soda, and stir. Pour the grenadine syrup along the inside edge of the bowl, and allow the red color to remain suspended in the yellow. Do not stir. As people ladle out drinks from the punch bowl, the colors will be mixed, but you can reestablish the sunrise effect when you replenish the bowl.

MENUS FOR YOUR KARAMU FEAST

Below are a few suggested menus. Feel free to add recipes of your own, or dishes contributed by your guests to create a wonderful feast.

Green Salad	Green Salad
Groundnut Stew	Roast Beef
Green Beans and Almonds	Green Beans and Almonds
Corn Bread	Zucchini Muffins
Ambrosia	Spiced Baked Apples
Chocolate Almond Cookies	Pineapple Sunrise Punch
Hot Apple Cider	

or   *or*

Fruit-in-Season Salad	Fruit-in-Season Salad
Spicy Black-eyed Peas and Rice	Tuna Sesame Salad
Candied Yams	Candied Yams
Corn Bread	Zucchini Muffins
Sugar Cookies	Chocolate Almond Cookies
Pineapple Sunrise Punch	Hot Apple Cider

or

THE
CHILDREN'S
BOOK OF
KWANZAA
....
134

CHAPTER SEVEN

SPECIAL PROGRAMS FOR KWANZAA

A good story is better than a good meal because it stays with you longer.
—Proverb

To enhance your Kwanzaa experience, you should have the opportunity to sing Kwanzaa songs, to recite Kwanzaa poems, and to tell and listen to Kwanzaa stories. Kwanzaa is a serious cultural experience, but it is also a festival. Take the time to share moments of laughter as well as to share solemn moments of reflection.

The story which follows is a story that can be told around the Kwanzaa table, or at the Karamu, or at a Girl or Boy Scout meeting. It can be read in the classroom, or on any occasion when you might want to have fun remembering the Nguzo Saba.

Also, with some simple modifications, this story can be performed as a play. You can build a leafy, plant-filled jungle set near a large blue patch of cloth to represent water. The actors can be children dressed in simple costumes and handmade animal masks. This play can also be performed in a puppet theater with the handmade puppets from chapter 5. Whatever you do, whether it is to recite poems you have written or play the part of a turtle in a Kwanzaa play, remember that one of the true goals of the Kwanzaa festival is to have fun.

BIP, BAM, BLIP, BOP, BANG, BOB, BOT, OR HOW THE ANIMALS HAD KWANZAA

All was not harmonious at the watering hole. The animals spent so much of their time fighting among themselves that there was rarely a moment of peace.

One day the hyena came to the watering hole, just a-jabbering and a-yelling. The other animals barely stopped arguing long enough to hear what he had to say. The hyena was shouting, "It's all coming to an end! It's all over! It's all done!" A sly little grin twisted his ghastly face. And then the hyena skulked away.

The animals who heard his words were mostly young ones. Babies, really, in the ways of the world. And every one of them interpreted the hyena's words as if the wretched animal were speaking in six different languages.

"He's talkin' about the locusts. The locusts are comin' and bringin' an end to the world," declared the monkey in a panic. "You know them insects can eat a fella out of house and home."

"Naw, it's a storm that's comin'," said the giraffe. "I can see the rain clouds up ahead. The rains will come and knock down all the best trees."

"I could drown in a rainstorm," said the turtle. "I can already hear the rolling waves and thunder. A flood like that could wash me into the sea."

"That's not it," said the ostrich, his words muffled because he was hiding his head in a hole in the ground. "That's the sound of lava flowing. From where I am, it's obvious there's a volcano about to blow."

"You're right about one thing," said the elephant. "That's smoke you're smelling. But it's a jungle fire I'm smelling with this trunk."

"Not one of you got a lick of sense," said the snake as he

fell out of the tree. "It's an earthquake that hyena was talking about, and I'm slithering right out of here, 'cause there's no bigger end to the world than the end of the world an earthquake brings."

There you have it. One simple hyena says six simple words and seven simple animals start acting simpleminded. They all raised their snouts, beaks, and lips in a chorus of hoots, hisses, buzzes, bangs, bips, burps, and buts.

"I think we should all dig a hole and hide our food underground," said the monkey. "That's the only way to avoid those greedy locusts."

"I think we should all find a cave and hide in it," said the giraffe. "That way we can all avoid that horrible storm that's coming."

"I think we should all start a stampede," said the turtle. "If we all run fast enough we can avoid that flood that's coming."

"I think we should climb up high in the trees," said the ostrich. "That has to be the only way we can save ourselves from the waves of lava from the volcano that's erupting."

"I think we should all just jump into the lake," said the elephant. "Is there any better way to avoid the fire that's coming?"

"If any of you all had an ounce of a brain," hissed the snake, "you'd realize there's nothin' you can do 'cause there's nothin' can stop the end of the world." And then all of the rest of the animals let out such a mass of pips, squeaks, booms, bams, plips, scitches, and splats that they woke up the ancient old lion.

"Rrrrrooooooaaaarrrrr," said the lion, more than a bit annoyed. "What on earth is all the commotion about?"

"Locusts are coming!" babbled the monkey.

"Storm's about to hit us!" screeched the giraffe.

"Here comes the flood!" screamed the turtle.

"Volcano's 'bout to blow!" twitched the ostrich.

"We'll all burn up!" thundered the elephant.

"World's ending!" rattled the snake.

"Well, if you don't quiet down, I will be ending the world for all of you," said the lion. "You've got to let me figure this out. We've got to take action. The first thing we must do is get some *Umoja.*"

"Umoja?" asked the elephant. "What's that, a big fan to blow the fire away?"

"No," growled the lion. "Umoja means 'unity.' We have to organize and think as one, or we won't be able to solve our problems."

"Well, the hyena says there's somethin' comin', and it's gonna mean our end," said the turtle.

"So if that's all we know," said the old lion carefully, "we will have to prepare ourselves for the very worst together, because only together are we at our full strength."

The animals all nodded their heads up and down, *bip, blam, bop, zang, zip, zim, sop.* "Yeah, we can do it. We can all do it, if we stay together."

"Rrroooaaarr!" bellowed the lion. "That's the ticket! And that happens to be the next step. *Kujichagulia.* We've determined that we can take care of ourselves!"

The rest of the animals all clanged tusks and beaks together, then slapped paws and scales and feathers and fur in agreement.

"The third step," said the lion, "is *Ujima,* collective work and responsibility. We've all got to work together to build up a defense against whatever's coming. If we work together, we can all build a shelter that will withstand any harm that could come."

"If we build it with a lot of leaves, it should keep the locusts away," said the monkey.

"If we build it nice and tall, it will keep us all dry in the rain," said the giraffe.

"If we build a wall around it, it should protect us from the floods," said the turtle.

"If we build it really strong, lava from the volcanoes will just flow around us," said the ostrich.

"If we build it away from other structures, we won't be crushed by earthquakes," said the snake.

"If we build it near the water, we can't be burned by fire," said the elephant.

"If we all build it together, it will be seven times as strong," said the lion, and they all began to work together.

All day long the animals gathered fallen tree branches, logs, and bamboo poles. They built a lean-to into the mouth of a cave near the watering hole, and reinforced it by sinking their poles deep in the ground. They dug a trench all around their shelter,  and then stacked rocks high to make a fence for protection. And then the animals all took a break at the side of the lake.

"What's next, Elder Lion?" asked the elephant. "Should we just go in the shelter, and hide away?"

"No, the fourth step is to practice *Ujamaa*, which means we should pool all our resources. We'll just have to work together to harvest as much food as we can. Then we can share what we have with one another if disaster comes."

"I don't know if I want to share my bananas with anyone," said the monkey. "I haven't seen anybody climbing trees for food but me."

"If we don't all share what each of us has, we all will suffer," said the turtle.

"Even with the monkey's bananas, there's still not enough food. We'll have to gather more," said the ostrich.

"Do you think we can work together long enough without fighting to get the job done? That's what hurt us in the past," said the elephant.

"Why don't you put your money where your trunk is," asked the snake, "and start helping us to gather some food?"

"You're right," said the elephant sheepishly. "I know I've stepped on a few toes in my time."

"And even I left my peanut shells wherever they fell," said the snake as he gathered roots.

"And I left the lake a filthy mess after my bath," said the giraffe as he gathered bananas.

"And I trampled all over the greenest plants," said the ostrich as he gathered plantains.

"Maybe we can clean up this mess we made and build our community back," said the elephant as he gathered yams.

"Maybe we can," agreed the lion. "That's called *Nia* or purpose. We must all play a part in restoring our community to greatness."

"Well, then, I think I can start by sharing my food," said the monkey.

"Good ape," hissed the snake as he wrapped himself in a hug around the monkey.

The lion roared in agreement. "That means the next step we need to practice is the principle of *Kuumba* or creativity. We must do things for one another. We can use all of our talents to create a better world."

"Good thing we have the wise old lion to go to for advice," said the turtle. "Or who knows what disaster could have befallen us."

"That's called *Imani*. Respect for the wisdom of our leaders," said the giraffe. "That's something else I've learned today."

After they had finished their work the ostrich said, "I'm gettin' a hankerin' for some fun. I can't think of anything

I'd rather do, if these really are the last few moments before the volcano blows, than play a little song for my good friends." He pulled out a guitar and started to strum a little song.

"I've got a little gift for you, too," said the elephant, "because if there's one thing I'd like to do in the last few moments before we all burn up, it's dance with you . . ." The elephant took the giraffe by the hoof, and waltzed her around the lakeside. The snake started to shake his rattles, and joined along with the happy beat. The turtle took out a kazoo he had under his shell, and began to honk out a happy melody. The monkey started to pull out some of the stores of food and arranged a wonderful array of food by the water's edge. There were coconuts, bananas, plantains, manioc—a veritable Kwanzaa Karamu. And the snake even put up some decorations. There were

flowers, and pictures, and posters from a time when the community was peaceful and happy and there was no fear. The animals did not worry about the end of the world because they knew that in a world that was unified, strong, and prepared, they could defeat anything that could harm them. They fell asleep where they last rested, snoring in a chorus of hoos, hees, snoos, snees, poos, honks, and hums.

The animals all awoke to the slow rumble of the hyena choking. "What are you all still doing here?" he stuttered. "Don't you fools know to run away from disaster?"

"We're ready for anything that's coming," chirped the chimp.

"We've unified with Umoja," said the turtle.

"We're determined with Kujichagulia," said the elephant.

"We're working together with Ujima," said the ostrich.

"We've got Nia—purpose to build for ourselves," said the monkey.

"We're creative," said snake. "We've got Kuumba."

"And the best thing of all, we've got Imani—faith in ourselves and in our elders," said the elephant. "'Cause if we hadn't listened to the old lion, we would have foolishly jumped in the lake. . . ."

"Climbed up a tree . . .," said the ostrich.

"Stampeded . . .," said the turtle.

"Hid in a cave . . .," said the giraffe.

"Dug a hole . . .," said the monkey.

"Or just slithered on out of here . . .," said the snake.

"Don't you idiots understand? That's what I wanted," said the hyena. "I said the world was gonna end because I wanted to keep this place all for myself. And you didn't even have the sense to run away."

"No," said the lion. "On the contrary. We had the sense not to allow one bad thing or person to destroy all the good things we have."

"Why don't you just sit that evil attitude down," said the monkey, "and share in the good life we have created here."

"Are you tellin' me you'll let me join you, even though I tried to do you harm?" asked the hyena.

"We're all brothers and sisters," said the lion. And wouldn't you know it, *bip, bam, blip, bop, bang, bob,* and *bot,* from that Kwanzaa festival on, the animals all pretty much got along.

CHAPTER EIGHT

HOW DO I PREPARE FOR KWANZAA?

Expectation comes before the dawn. But preparation brings the sun up.
—Proverb

If Kwanzaa seems like a ceremony and an institution you want to make a part of your life, it's important that you start planning early. You should determine whether you want to celebrate in your home with your family, in your school, in your community, or just by yourself. You should determine how much of the preparation can be accomplished by yourself, and how much another child, like a brother or sister, or an adult, like a parent or teacher, can help you with this project.

If this is your first Kwanzaa, you probably will have to start from scratch. But this should be a lot of fun for you, because you help establish the traditions that your family or school will carry on for years.

When you prepare for Kwanzaa, you must first ask permission from your parents and talk to them about the kind of celebration you would like your family to observe. Perhaps your father or mother would like to have a candlelighting ceremony

every evening and pass gifts just between members of the family. If that is the case, then it would only be necessary for you or your family to buy or make the implements of Kwanzaa, make or buy your gifts, and then have a family dinner together on the sixth day for the Karamu. If you would like to have a big Karamu feast to which you would invite guests, this will require additional planning.

Perhaps you would like to celebrate Kwanzaa with your school class or Scout troop. After getting permission from your teacher or troop leader, you again would have to determine what kind of Kwanzaa you want to celebrate.

Do you want to purchase a Kinara, Mkeka, unity cup, and the other symbols from a store and share them with the rest of the members of your troop? Or do you want to make every part of your Kwanzaa celebration by hand, from candles to invitations to gifts, and take what you have made home to share with your family? Or do you want to make Kwanzaa crafts to sell at a bazaar you organize to raise money for some project in the community? Once you have determined what kind of celebration you want to observe, you can plan the time, materials, and skills you will need with the help of an adult.

First you should analyze which of your projects will take the longest to create. If you want to make *everything* from scratch, including, let's say, the kente cloth wall hanging, you will have to start work five or six weeks in advance. Most of the other crafts will not take five to six weeks to create, but it would be a good idea for you and your family to decide by the middle of fall, say by the month of October, whether you will be observing Kwanzaa and how much of your celebration will be handmade.

I have included a calendar form for you to fill out to plan your holiday. I have also included the approximate time the different crafts should take. Make photocopies of the calendar, and fill in the copies according to what tasks you need to accomplish. Then draw a line through each task as you complete it. If you follow this plan and fulfill your tasks as specified, you should be able to create a handmade, fun-filled, well-planned Kwanzaa holiday!

The following are suggested time schedules you should consider when you plan to make crafts for Kwanzaa. When three weeks are suggested for making a Kinara, that does not mean that the craft will take twenty-one days. It simply means that getting the supplies and putting together that item might take a bit more time than other crafts. If you start and finish making a handcrafted Kinara earlier than the other crafts, you will have time to finish everything on your list. If, however, all you plan to do is make one simple Kinara for Kwanzaa, you could probably accomplish that goal in six to eight hours' time over two days.

IF YOU PLAN TO MAKE	START
Needlework	6 weeks before Kwanzaa
Mkeka	4 weeks before Kwanzaa
Kinara	3 weeks before Kwanzaa
Candles	3 weeks before Kwanzaa
All Papier-mâché Crafts	2 weeks before Kwanzaa
Musical Instruments	2 weeks before Kwanzaa
Gathering the Muhindi, Tambiko, and Mazao	1 week before Kwanzaa

IF YOU PLAN TO HAVE A KARAMU FEAST WITH GUESTS	START
Make Invitations	4 weeks before Kwanzaa
Mail Invitations	3 weeks before Kwanzaa
Plan Menu	1 week before Kwanzaa
Buy Groceries	December 29—2 days before
Start Cooking	December 29—2 days before

IN CONCLUSION

I hope this book will help you to create a Kwanzaa that is a true "Celebration of Family, Community and Culture," as Dr. Karenga envisioned so many years ago. I hope it will also keep you working toward ways to make your life, and the lives of those around you, better.

CHAPTER NINE

WHERE TO BUY

The end of the road is only the start to another's journey.

—Proverb

The following is a list of possible sources for your arts and crafts supplies. Most of the crafts described in chapters 4 and 5 are designed to use materials that are readily found in most homes or classrooms. But there may be materials that you will need to buy.

The following is a list of suppliers indicating what they sell and a toll-free telephone number (where available) that you can call to obtain their catalogs or locate the store nearest you. Some suppliers do not have retail stores and only sell arts and crafts supplies through catalogs. I have indicated how you might obtain those catalogs, and their cost, if there is one. Happy Kwanzaa shopping!

ARTS AND CRAFTS RETAILERS

For a wide variety of craft supplies sold in stores located all over the nation, call for the store nearest you:

Michaels Arts & Crafts Stores
1–800–MICHAELS

LUMBER AND HARDWARE RETAILERS

For lumber, tools, wood turnings. Check you own phone directory for the store nearest you:

Home Base
Home Depot

FIVE-AND-DIME STORES

For some crafts supplies, including needlework, look in your telephone directory for the retail store closest to you.

Newberry
TG&Y
McCrory
McLellan
Kress
Kmart
Woolworth

CATALOG ARTS AND CRAFTS SUPPLIERS

A tremendous variety of school and arts and crafts supplies can be ordered by catalog. Use the toll-free numbers listed below to call for catalogs, or request them by mail when no number is available.

United Art and Education Supply Co., Inc.
P.O. Box 9219
Fort Wayne, IN 46899
Request their free catalog on school letterhead

Triarco Arts and Crafts Inc.
Plymouth, MN
1-800-328-3360 (in Minnesota: 1-800-635-9361)

THE
CHILDREN'S
BOOK OF
KWANZAA
....
150

Art Depot Discount Art Supplies
Grand Junction, CO
1-800-782-5243

S & S Arts and Crafts
Colchester, CT
1-800-243-9232

Nasco Arts & Crafts
write to 901 Janesville Avenue
Fort Atkinson, WI 53538-0901
for free catalog

Sax Arts & Crafts
write to Visual Art Resources
P.O. Box 51710
New Berlin, WI 53131
for free catalog

J. L. Hammett Company
Service to Educators
Montclair, CA
Phoenix, AZ
Overland Park, KS
1-800-333-4600

ART SUPPLIES

An extensive selection of art supplies that can be ordered by
catalog by using the following toll-free numbers:

Discount Art Supply
Denver, CO
1-800-737-3997

Daniel Smith Artists' Materials
Seattle, WA
1-800-426-6740

Utrecht Art Supply
Brooklyn, NY
1-800-223-9132

Co-Op Artists' Materials
(includes Binders Discount Art Centers)
Atlanta, GA
1-800-877-3242

Dick Blick
Galesburg, IL
1-800-447-8192

AFRICAN FABRICS

The Unique Spool
For a catalog send a large self-adressed
    stamped envelope to:
407 Corte Majorca
Vacaville, CA 95688

Batiks, Etc.
Send $5 for fabric samples to:
411 Pine Street
Fort Mill, SC 29715

Fabrics & Findings
Rochester, NY
1-800-527-CRAFT

THE
CHILDREN'S
BOOK OF
KWANZAA
....
152

Nu Nubian
Downey, CA
1–800–982–7000 for a catalog

MISCELLANEOUS CATALOG SUPPLIERS

For leather and jewelry crafts from retail stores found nationwide:
Tandy Leather Company
1–800–821–0801

For jewelry crafts catalog:
River Gems & Findings
Albuquerque, NM
1–800–443–6766

For a candle-making supply catalog send a large self-addressed
   stamped envelope to:
Pourette Manufacturing Co.
P.O. Box 15220
Seattle, WA 98115

GLOSSARY

BENDERA YA TAIFA—The black, red, and green African American unity flag designed by Marcus Garvey.

EMANCIPATION PROCLAMATION—Document signed January 1, 1863, which declared "all persons held as slaves within any State, or designated part of the State, the people whereof shall be in rebellion against the United States, shall be then, thenceforward, and forever free."

HABARI GANI? (ha-BAR-ee GON-ee)—Means "What's new?" in Kiswahili. The reply should be the Kwanzaa principle of that particular day. For example, the first day's reply should be "Umoja."

HARAMBEE (ha-RAM-bee)—Means "Let's pull together" in Kiswahili.

IMANI (ee-MAH-nee)—Faith. The seventh principle of the Nguzo Saba.

JIM CROW—Rules of conduct, particularly in the South, which restricted the rights of and segregated African Americans.

KARENGA, DR. MAULANA ("RON")—Founder of the holiday Kwanzaa in 1966. He is currently professor and chair of black studies at the California State University at Long Beach, and the executive director of the Institute of Pan-African Studies.

KINARA (kee-NAH-rah)—Candleholder used during the Kwanzaa celebration which represents the African ancestors.

KISWAHILI (kee-swa-HEE-lee)—The language most commoly spoken on the African continent, often referred to as Swahili (Swahili actually refers to the people of the region, while Kiswahili is the language the people speak). It is the language used by Dr. Karenga to name the principles and components of the Kwanzaa holiday.

KUJICHAGULIA (koo-jee-chah-goo-LEE-ah)—Self-determination. The second principle of Kwanzaa.

KUUMBA (koo-OOM-bah)—Creativity. The sixth principle of the Nguzo Saba.

KWANZAA (KWAN-za)—An African American cultural holiday, originated by Dr. Maulana Karenga, celebrated annually between December 26 and January 1.

MAZAO (mah-ZAH-oh)—The crops, symbolized by a basket of fruit and vegetables at the Kwanzaa celebration, which represent the rewards of labor.

MISHUMAA SABA (mee-shoo-MAH SAH-ba)—The seven candles used in the Kwanzaa celebration which represent the Nguzo Saba, the Seven Principles of Kwanzaa.

MKEKA (m-KAY-kah)—A straw mat used at the Kwanzaa celebration to represent tradition.

MUHINDI (moo-HEEN-dee)—The corn which represents the children in the family or community during the Kwanzaa celebration.

NIA (NEE-ah)—Purpose. The fifth principle of the Nguzo Saba.

NGUZO SABA (n-GOO-za SAH-ba)—The Seven Principles of Kwanzaa: unity, self-determination, collective work and responsibility, cooperative economics, purpose, creativity, and faith.

PAPIER-MÂCHÉ (PAY-per ma-SHAY)—French for "chewed up paper." Process of covering paper or paper pulp with glue to build up a form which can be used as a sculptural or crafts structure.

RECONSTRUCTION—The period after the Civil War, between 1865 and 1877, in which the former slave gained some rights in the rebuilding of the Union. But the rights were quickly taken away, particularly in the South.

TAMSHI LA TUTAONANA (TAM-shi la tu-ta-u-NA-na)—The Farewell Statement read at the Karamu on the sixth day of the Kwanzaa celebration.

UJAMAA (oo-ja-MAH)—Collective economics. The fourth principle of the Nguzo Saba.

UJIMA (oo-JEE-mah)—Collective work and responsiblity. The third principle of the Nguzo Saba.

UMOJA (oo-MOH-jah)—Unity. The first principle of the Nguzo Saba.

THIRTEENTH AMENDMENT—Amendment to the Constitution of the United States, ratified in December 1865, which abolished slavery.

UNDERGROUND RAILROAD—A series of safe houses and hiding places that led escaping slaves North and to Canada, where slavery had been abolished.

ZAWADI (za-WAH-dee)—Gifts.

BIBLIOGRAPHY

Bennett, Lerone, Jr. *Before the* Mayflower: *A History of Black America*. 4th ed. Chicago: Johnson Publishing Co., 1969.

Blue, Rose, and Corinne Naden. *Barbara Jordan, Politician*. New York: Chelsea House Publishers, 1990.

Casselman, B.J. *Crafts from around the World*. New York: Meredith Corp. Creative Home Library in association with *Better Homes and Gardens*, 1975.

"Colin Powell, Superstar." *U.S. News & World Report*, 20 September 1993, 51.

Everett, Cheryl, Susan Wells, and Evelyn White. *The African Americans*. Edited by Charles M. Collins and David Cohen. New York: Viking Studio Books, 1993.

Franklin, John Hope, and Alfred A. Moss. *From Slavery to Freedom, A History of Negro Americans*. 6th ed. New York: McGraw-Hill Publishing, 1988.

Hughes, Langston and Milton Meltzer. *A Pictorial History of the Negro in America*. 3rd revised ed. Revised and augmented by C. Eric Lincoln and Milton Meltzer. New York: Crown Publishers, 1968.

Jakoubek, Robert. *Martin Luther King, Jr., Civil Rights Leader.* New York: Chelsea House Publishers, 1989.

Karenga, Maulana. *The African American Holiday of Kwanzaa, A Celebration of Family, Community, and Culture.* Los Angeles: University of Sankore Press, 1988.

Lindsey, Howard O. *A History of Black America.* Secaucus, NJ: Chartwell Books, 1985, 1993.

Long, Richard A. *African Americans: A Portrait.* New York, Avenel, NJ: Crescent Books, 1985, 1993.

McClester, Cedric. *Kwanzaa, Everything You Always Wanted to Know but Didn't Know Where to Ask.* New York: Gumbs & Thomas Publishers, 1985.

Newman, Thelma R. *Contemporary African Arts and Crafts.* New York: Crown Publishers, 1974.

"Peanut Butter—A Stirring Tale." *Los Angeles Times.* 20 March 1994.

Pohanca, Brian C. *Distant Thunder—A Photographic Essay on the American Civil War.* Charlottesville, VA: Thomasson–Grant, 1988.

Robinson, Wilhelmina S. *International Library of Afro-American Life and History.* Cornwell Heights, PA: Publishers Agency, 1976.

Rogers, J.A. *World's Great Men of Color.* 1947. New York: Collier Macmillan, 1972.

Salley, Columbus. *The Black 100: A Ranking of the Most Influential African-Americans, Past and Present.* Secaucus, NJ: Carol Publishing Group, Citadel Press, 1993.

Senna, Carl. *Colin Powell, a Man of War and Peace.* New York: Walker & Company, 1992.

KWANZAA PLANNING

MONTH OF _____

SUNDAY	MONDAY	TUESDAY	WEDNESDAY	THURSDAY	FRIDAY	SATURDAY